THE COCK ROAD GANG
(The story of the Caines family)

By

IAN S. BISHOP

All rights reserved. No part of this book may be reproduced, stored in a retrieval system, or transmitted in any form or by any means, electronic, mechanical, photocopying, recording or otherwise, without the prior permission in writing from the Author.

Copyright 2003 Ian S. Bishop

In preparing this book I have received the generous assistance from my wife Doreen, and my special thanks go to her for her help and encouragement during its preparation and sale. I am also extremely grateful to our close friend Sheila Brooks for reading and helping to correct the proofs, and to Mrs. Greta Pearce for allowing me to quote from copy letters and documents she had in her possession, as part of her family history research. Throughout this book I have endeavoured to minimize any mistakes made but, should any exist then unfortunately they are of my own making, for which I apologize and trust that any such errors will not distract you, from enjoying the contents of this book.

Ian S. Bishop   September 2003

Printed by Adlard Print & Reprographics Ltd
The Old School, The Green, Ruddington,
Nottingham, NG11 6HH.

Tel: 0115 921 4863 Fax: 0115 945 6474 ISDN: 0115 846 1338

Website: www.adlardprint.com Email info@adlardprint.com

Before considering the make-up and understanding the particular features of the *Cock Road Gang,* it is necessary to look at the times in which they lived and the environment in which they were brought up, and to try not to pre-judge them with twenty-first century morals and opinions. The period covered by this book is roughly the one hundred and ten year period from 1727 to 1837, and is based around the parishes of Bitton and Oldland, but events occurred outside of those parishes, some many miles away, and a number of participants lived in the adjoining parishes of Hanham, Kingswood, Warmley and Syston.

Life for many people, and in particular the working class, was harsh to say the least, and revolved around a great deal of hard work, a minimal amount of money which might or might not be sufficient to scrape together enough sustenance to be able to eke out an existence, poor unsanitary living conditions, with no medical or State Welfare, and little or no comfort to break up the boredom and drudgery of their existence. Obviously there was a certain degree of recreation for those who would and could seek them, but mostly they were for men, and revolved around drinking, gambling and pleasures of the flesh, all of which had a detrimental affect on their families, as what little money was earned could soon disappear in an alehouse, or some such other establishment. As for the womenfolk, life consisted of continued hard work, keeping house, bearing children, and trying to put food on the table to feed her hungry brood, whilst at the same time, juggling with the need to look after her husband, plus of course the endless drudgery of washing and cleaning, although she did try to make the most of the occasional trips to market, meeting up with old friends, and catching up with the local gossip.

The establishment of authority in eighteenth century England was complex, uneven in its impact and effectiveness, and fundamentally controlled by the establishment, to benefit themselves, and to protect their own property, without any balance of fairness, compassion or social conscience. Throughout the whole country there were men who had the legal right, by status and/or economical strength to rule over other men, effectively meaning that there was always one man who could lord it over many other men, and their standard of existence was totally dependant upon how philanthropic that one man was. For many years there were large swaths of the country where formal institutions of authority were relatively new and certainly not deep-rooted in the midsts of time and as such were very much less respected, causing the cement of a modern civilisation to remain in its fluid form. Where there had been an accepted form of law and order for hundreds of years, the populace had grown to accept the authority from whence it came, with the rules being handed down from one generation to another, but in those other areas the people remained less cultured and much more independent.

For hundreds of years the area covered by this book was literary the King's Wood, and as such there were austere rules which governed what could or could not be done within the forest boundary. However there were always a few who would risk everything for food, for plunder, for escape as with such a large area to police, and a relatively small number of constables to carry out the King's authority, the chances of being caught were not particularly high, especially as the Sovereign's interest in maintaining the forest for his own sole use began to wane. Prisoners on the run from other authorities could use the forest as a place to seek shelter, and the destitute could use the forest as a comparatively safe place to squat and live, whilst the forest bounty could be purloined, making the area an extremely attractive place for social rejects and those who felt that law and order was not for them. The exercise of parochial authority, be it from the upper classes in the form of the "lord of the Manor", and/or land owning employers, or from the established church, was either non existent or at its very best extremely weak, and as the royal use of the forest changed, but more importantly waned during the seventeenth and eighteenth centuries, then much more of the space was occupied by groups of people whose basic principles in life were a general lack of authority, and unruliness. On the one hand there were those would be entrepreneurs who had the wealth and position in society to step outside the law, lay claim to an area of the forest and have the audacity of adopting for themselves, the land and mineral rights already held in the name of a valid noble, calling those areas "Liberties", thus openly flouting age old legalities. On the other hand there were those who were prepared to sweat and toil for their aforementioned masters, for a pittance, whilst taking most if not all the risks, of death, injury or prosecution. During the seventeenth century, a number of lawsuits took place, which undoubtedly caused a great deal of inconvenience and no doubt a certain amount of financial loss to the claimants, but which almost assuredly left the workers out of a job, and possibly in prison, with no money to feed their family or themselves. In addition, the colliers were prevented from taking, and using for their own benefit, the coal privileges previously granted to them.

Further attempts were also made by Parliament at the Crowns bidding, to prevent more encroachments in the forest, which inevitably led to civil unrest, and ultimately to full blown riots taking place. Such civil disturbance lasted for a number of weeks but with the king anxious to raise more money for his own ambitious plans, for the divine "Right of Kings", the pressure to enforce the law of the land dwindled and anarchy reigned, allowing the claimants to restart their exploitation of the forest and its wealth both above and below ground. As the years rolled by, the trees in the Chase declined by such a rate that by around the 1690's they had all but disappeared, and thus the forest-dwellers became more and more unconstrained by institutional authority, and set up their own rules of conduct, and rules of honour. In doing so they created a distinct form of culture and existence, which was frequently at odds with the more established rule of law and conduct. Although they had chosen to live this way, there is no doubt that their life in general was particularly harsh, which in turn toughened and hardened those involved, leading them to acquire a notoriety for being hard fighters who had little or no respect for the normal conventions of life.

Such changes to these groups of people was not confined to Kingswood, with copious forest-dwellers in many parts of the country going down similar paths, with numerous common features independently acquired. Men of certain occupations stood out amongst the majority, being noted for their independence, and strong feeling of injustice, and one of the occupations to the fore were the coalminers, in whatever location they lived.

Illness and death was always in close proximity with the poor quality of basic food products and water, which was further exacerbated by there being a complete lack of hygiene, thus even the simple task of washing one's hands before preparing food was, in the main, considered unnecessary and more often than not was either forgotten or simply ignored, especially as all the water used and/or consumed in the house had to be fetched from a communal well or nearby stream, and soap was expensive. In addition there were the extremely poor working conditions to take into consideration at a time when the value of his workforce was, more often than not, not that high on the employer's list of priorities.

Many worked for the various mine owners whose main precedence in life was to get the coal to the market place as cheaply as possible, and then to sell the coal at the best possible price, thus the workforce was naturally a means to an end. Both men and boys worked underground in the Kingswood area, in extremely difficult conditions, very often being lowered into and out of the pit on a thick rope, attached to which were loops of thinner rope that passed around the miner's thighs to create a form of seat. Thus by holding onto the main rope with one hand, and sitting around that same rope, a group of ten or twelve men with boys could descend into the eternal darkness together, strung like onions on a truss. During the descent, which was almost certainly made in complete darkness, once they had descended fifteen feet or so and lost the benefit of the daylight above them, the miners would need to use their free hand to steady the rope and themselves. This was the only way of avoiding being dashed, from an erratic pendulum, against the unlined ragged sides of the shaft, and/or to just stop themselves from being blindly swung around, On many occasions, fathers or elder brothers would carry their 6-10 year old son/brother on their back as they reached out to grab the rope that was hanging in the middle of the eight foot wide shaft, knowing that just one slip could send them both hurtling to certain death some five or more hundred feet below. Understandably, some of the smaller children, especially when it was the first time that they were due to go underground, would become very agitated and frightened, and concerned that they would struggle and let go of their hold, it was no unknown for the father to put his son in a sack with the open end closed and held over his back, before reaching out for his own hold on the rope. Once at the bottom of the shaft, the men and boys would strip to the waist and remove their shoes and stockings, if worn, all to be set in small pathetic piles at the foot of the shaft, before stooping/crawling on hands and knees to the coalface and the start of a 12-14 hour shift.

It has been said that many of the mine owners had little regard for the men and boys who toiled and died so that they, the mine owners, could maintain a standard of living vastly improved upon that enjoyed by their employees, and on one occasion their attitude was clearly expressed in public. At one of *Mr. SAMUEL WHITTUCK'S* mines, a small group of tired miners crawled their way back to the bottom of the shaft, having just endured a fourteen-hour shift, at or near the coalface. Most of them had just one train of thought, which was to reach the top, and to breathe in the fresh night air, before walking to their respective homes, and the prospects of a hot meal. At the bottom of the shaft, they tried to brush off as much of the day's grime as possible, before dressing, and then climbing onto the rope, giving a signal each time the rope had to be raised six feet or so to let on the next man. With the last man on, there was a period of four to five minutes before they would be able to feel the fresh night air spilling over the rim of the shaft, and then with luck a further two or three minutes whilst each man was able to step across the chasm onto the surface, and then a tired walk home.

The first four minutes or so seemed quite normal to their aching limbs, although on one or two occasions the rope slipped back slightly as though it may have been stretching, but none of the tired men took any real notice, as they tried to stop themselves from rotating. At the top of the rope, the first man shivered slightly as the cold night air reached his body, which had for the past fourteen hours adapted to the constant temperature of the mine, and the sweat of his toil. As he took his first gulp of fresh air and noticed the starlit sky framed by the rim of the shaft, the rope around the windlass broke, and with nothing to save them, all five men were dashed against the wall of the shaft as they hurtled to the floor below; amidst flailing arms and legs, all five men died together.

At the subsequent inquest, an experienced rope maker told the jury that, having studied the sample of rope taken from the scene of the incident, he was forced to conclude that he had never before seen rope being used, which was in such bad condition; adding a rider, that he had better quality rope brought into his yard as "old junk". In giving their verdict, the jury censured the owner, Samuel Whittuck, and his mine manager, for neglect in not ensuring that the equipment being used was of good quality. However laudable the criticism might have been, it did little or nothing to improve the working conditions in the mines, and no real or financial compensation for the relatives. It did however provoke a response from the mine owner in the local newspaper, who published a letter received from Mr Samuel Whittuck that refuted the criticism, and was couched in language which clearly attempted to vindicate himself from all blame, claiming that he could not possibly be held responsible for the tragedy on the grounds that:

"so little do I concern myself with the works that I seldom go there"

Strangely he seemed more than happy to accept the profits, if not the responsibility, which of course fell squarely on the shoulders of none other than his mine manager, although as far as can be determined, the manager retained his job, whilst five families had to cope with the loss of their prime bread-winner.

Although this was just one incident used to highlight the conditions and attitudes under which many worked, it is also necessary to put into context the fact that the average collier earned just under 10/- [50p] for a 70 hour week, and that this level of income had hardly changed for twelve or more years. In contrast the price of bread, which at the time was a major part of the workingman's staple diet, had risen to 1/- [05p] per quartern loaf, thus one weeks requirement of around three 2lb loaves was costing the family around thirty per cent of the collier's earnings, which in today's context would mean that around £75 was being spent on bread alone, no wonder those who were resourceful would try and find other ways of augmenting their family budget.

Time has been spent on describing the terrible conditions endured by those who were coal workers, but whilst a large proportion of the population in the area covered were so employed, many found work on the land, as well as there being a multitude of minor jobs from pin making to the brass industry, to sundry work as exotic as "oyster sellers". However diverse the eighteenth century workforce was, what linked them together was bad pay, poor working conditions, poor housing, and extreme poverty and squalor, bound up in a deep frustration that life and the upper classes were determined to keep them in their place, and under their thumb.

******

Such was the ingrained feeling of injustice, and the inbred desire that the collective argument should be backed up with violence, particularly within certain sections of the community, that the miners from the many pits in the area soon created for themselves a reputation for being troublesome, rowdy and lawless, much of which could be traced back to the early part of the eighteenth century when there was a series of bad harvests which greatly increased the price of all basic foodstuffs. Food had never been particularly cheap, and these increases simply added to the intolerable and miserable state of those workers and their families that lived in the area collectively known as Kingswood. Once again there were those who were very hungry and those who were not so hungry because they could either afford the higher prices, or because as agricultural workers they may have had a better opportunity to obtain the farmer's scraps. Accordingly a fight for survival was inevitable with those at the bottom of the pile deciding collectively without consultation to fight back and take the law into their own hands by carrying out acts of petty theft and robbery. Unfortunately, as these crimes increased the situation within the community worsened as many of the victims were in fact the same people who were suffering the affects of the high food prices, and accordingly crime played upon crime with all involved ending up as losers, including of course, those who suffered in silence with their own level of personal dignity keeping them going through those most trying times.

There were, during September 1729, a number of disturbances in east Bristol particularly amongst the local weavers who collectively decided, that they needed to strengthen their resolve by bringing in outside help, and knowing the reputation of the miners it was decided that they should walk to Kingswood to meet up and exchange thoughts and views and share opinions about the behaviour and actions of their respective employers, no doubt over a pint or two of Kingswood's finest ale. At that meeting they unanimously agreed to take action by demonstrating their disgust at the treatment meted out by the upper classes only ever interested in looking after their own financial welfare and social status. If we are to be treated as scum, then scum we shall be was the prevailing attitude as they marshalled their joint force together to march back to Bristol. In taking this particular stance, the miners of Kingswood were demonstrating their support for their fellow workers, although cynics might claim that it was just a good excuse for the hooligan element of the miners to get into a fight.

Over the years, the reputation of the Kingswood miner for being uncouth, hard fighting, resolute ruffians with complete contempt for the law grew and grew, and quite often they were called upon or volunteered to go to one demonstration or another. The deficient availability and high price of wheat in 1753 caused more problems, and on the 21 May, hundreds of men from the Kingswood coalfield rallied to the city through Lawford's Gate, and then onto the Council House where, together with many of Bristol's citizens, they put their case as forcibly as possible to the Mayor and Aldermen. Having then been told that their grievances would be looked into, the majority of the crowd expressed themselves satisfied. However, the miners and their cohorts were not that easily persuaded, and decided that they would underline their grievance and hunger by repatriating English corn which was currently on a ship at the quay bound for Dublin. There then proceeded a running battle between the constables, armed with staves, which they used indefensibly and with indecent force against the crowd, the militant miners and weavers, plus the innocent bystanders who had just simply become caught up in the melee. After a relatively brief encounter with the constables, the men from Kingswood withdrew, taking with them some who had been quite badly beaten, and leaving others who had been taken prisoner by the constables. Hearing of the treatment meted out to their colleagues, those miners who had been prepared to go home without a fight, now went to their friends' aid. As a result the running battle nearly turned into a full-blown riot, with many of the nearby property being vandalized and having windows smashed from thrown missiles.

Injuries abounded on both sides, and it was left to the somewhat bruised and battered miners to gradually leave the city, and head back for home with what spoils they could carry, and welcomed applications of vinegar and brown paper. Although their heads hurt, their hearts cried out for vengeance, sufficiently loud enough for their threats to be taken seriously by the local authority that they quickly gave instructions for a militia to be raised, and a number of citizens were enrolled as special constables. With both groups of men armed with muskets, they met outside Lawford's Gate on the 24 May, and on taking the fight to the mob, the better military trained men won the day and soon the militants had dispersed into small groups that broke up and disappeared into the surrounding countryside.

Not to be outdone, the Kingswood miners, who included from the Bitton/Oldland Common area, *EDWARD PEACOCK* (alias Peake), *RICHARD HOBBS; HENRY LEWIS; JACOB FORTER; MOSES ISLES; WILLIAM FRY,* and *GEORGE THOMPSON,* were back the following day and, together with hordes of weavers and numerous disorderly ruffians from the out parish of St Philip's, in total around 900, decided on a slightly different strategy and entered the city by way of Milk Street and advanced to Bridewell where one of Monday's rioters was being detained, awaiting trial. Despite the subsequent adversity of having one of their colleagues shot dead by one of the warders, the prison defences soon gave way and the mob piled in and began to ransack the building. However, with the main aim of the attack being the release of the prisoner soon dealt with, the next consideration in the mind of the miners was how to extricate themselves from their predicament, particularly now that a small troop of dragoons had turned up, and had immediately begun to fire quite indiscriminately over the heads of the rioters. With a certain degree of panic setting in, the fugitives broke up into small parties and began to scatter out of any hole that seemed safe to do so. Inevitably this soon led to there being numerous minor skirmishes taking place in and out of the narrow alleyways with a constant drive towards the anticipated safety of Lawford's Gate and beyond. One group of more dedicated and ruthless miners decided to take hostages with them, as possible protection for their own safety, and in the melee they managed to hold onto no less than six gentlemen, of whom three were rescued by the militia as the perpetrators tried to break-out of the city at Lawford's Gate. As far as the other three gentlemen were concerned, they found themselves being jostled and physically persuaded to take the Kingswood road, from where they were unceremoniously marched up the hill and beyond to a little used pit known to the miners. Once there, they were invited to descend underground into the dark damp bottom of the old shaft, where they remained for a number of days before they were eventually released, unharmed but no doubt mentally scarred. Back in the city on the day of the attack on the Bridewell, four colliers were dead, in excess of fifty were wounded, some of whom would later die of their wounds, and around thirty-five were being held captive.

Although it may appear from the above that the colliers, and other workers from the Kingswood area always came together in unison to meet head-on what they considered to be just causes, intermingled with a little bit of personal crime on the way, there were many more instances where perhaps just two or three men operated in concert with each other, which again may be a basis for the outsiders, and for the law enforcers to presume that a pseudo gang existed. For example, in 1781 *JOHN READ* and *JOHN WARD* both of whom were working colliers, and lived in the Oldland Common area, were condemned to death by a judge at Gloucester, having been indicted with the crime of housebreaking, and found guilty of the charge. At their trial, the prosecution described the accused men as being, part of a desperate gang who terrorised the good people of Bitton and the surrounding area, and that this same gang had long infested the County. Both men went to the scaffold and the long drop above the gatehouse at Gloucester Prison, on the 30th March 1781, and with their bodies being collected by their families the following day, they were buried on the north side of St Mary's churchyard on the 1st April 1781.

Two years later on the 1st September 1783, *JAMES BRYANT* of Bitton was executed for sheep stealing, whilst during the early part of that October, *BENJAMIN WEBB* and *GEORGE WARD,* also from the Bitton area were apprehended and committed to Tewkesbury Gaol having been charged with the theft and killing of two lambs the property of *ISAAC LEWIS* of Bitton. Although no explanation as to why they carried out this action is recorded in the trial script, it is reasonable to presume that it was to be shared out amongst family and friends, for a small monetary contribution, to give those families the chance of having for once, meat on their plate. Obviously from Mr Lewis' point of view, these were villains who had no right to his property let alone his profit, and accordingly took the matter of the theft quite seriously by posting a £20 reward (almost a whole year's income for those families starved of meat in their humdrum diet) for the capture and apprehension of the culprits. It is not clear whether the reward did the trick or whether there were other reasons behind the arrest of Benjamin and George, but when caught they were also found to be in the possession of two stolen horses. Having benefited from the home comforts of Tewkesbury Prison for two or three weeks, both men were transferred to Gloucester to stand trial at the next available quarter session, which was likely to be the Lent Quarter of 1784. Thus throughout the bitter winter of 1783/84, the men from Bitton languished in a damp, numbing, dark cell, with nothing other than lice ridden straw on which to lie, which had been thrown in to cover their excrement and that of the other inhabitants, both human and rodent. Certainly leg irons, which were designed to make it difficult to move, shackled both Webb and Ward to the wall of the cell, and were an absolute nuisance when the indigenous rats became too friendly and began gnawing at their feet.

Christmas must have been very good to them as it somehow brought a number of unexpected presents to both men, for they had mysteriously obtained/purloined a number of lock-picking implements, and saws, and understandably being tired of the hospitality afforded them by the gaol authorities, they succeeded by the New Year to have sawn through their leg irons, and were about to discard the metal from their extremely painful ulcerated legs, when they were unexpectedly visited by the Keeper of the Gaol, who having carried out an inspection, and physical search, found the damaged shackles, and implements, and ordered the men out of the cell. Determined that they should not be more successful in any future attempts to escape, Benjamin Webb and George Ward were taken to another cell and there they were secured by the application of several fetters colloquially known as *"The Widows Arms,"* which leaves little to the imagination and which must have been excruciatingly uncomfortable if not extremely painful, and very inhibiting.

Removed from the prison cell in March, the men appeared before the Lent Assizes, and were quickly found guilty and sentenced to death by hanging, a verdict that was carried out on the 26th March 1784. Two days later, their bodies were collected from the prison mortuary, and carried back to be buried at St Mary's Bitton.

In April 1786, two more men from the Bitton area, *JOSEPH FRY* and *SAMUEL WARD* were hanged at Gloucester prison for some minor misdemeanours, whilst *GEORGE FRY* was found guilty of burglary, condemned to death, but this was for some reason or another commuted to transportation for life.

During April 1795, two men acting on behalf of the local bailiff, called at a house in Kingswood, for the collection of outstanding rent, or goods to the value thereof. Within a very short space of time, the property was surrounded by an angry group of colliers, who considered that the bailiff's men needed to be taught a lesson, and accordingly they were marched off to a nearby pit, and there they were invited to descend to the bottom of the shaft and admire the miners' handiwork. For the next three or fours hours, the bailiffs were allowed, in the pitch-blackness, to contemplate their earlier actions, before being brought back up to the surface, where they were regaled with plentiful supplies of gin and gingerbread. Although the two men believed that they had seen all they could at the bottom of the shaft, the colliers were not quite so sure, and accordingly lowered the men back down to the bottom, and then left the pit and returned home. After a good nights sleep, the colliers returned to the pit, and for the second time in twenty-four hours, hauled the damp, and somewhat uncomfortable bailiff's men to the surface. However, they were to suffer further indignity when the miners demanded that they should each pay the colliers 3/- (0.15p) for their lodgings and sustenance, and swear an oath not to trouble the colliers and/or their friends again.

ABRAHAM ISLES, from Bitton, who was also frequently known by his friends and acquaintances as either Scram-handed Jemmy on account of him being left-handed, or as Twink, but there is no explanation why, together with *ABRAHAM SCULL* also from Bitton, plus *ROBERT WEBB* from Chippenham, but with family connections to Oldland, walked to Pensford on the 10th May 1799, and there stole three horses. Having then ridden the animals up the hill out of the village, they soon reached the turnpike house at Chelwood, where Abraham Isles asked for change as he only had a shilling with which to pay the toll. This meant that the toll keeper's wife had to go back into her house, and into a small room where she kept a bureau in which money was retained. With her back turned, and her husband working away in the fields, Webb and Scull dismounted and followed the defenceless old woman into the house, and brandishing a pistol robbed her of all the money in the bureau, amounting to around £5. (equivalent to about £2,200 by today's values) Whilst this was going on, Isles sat quietly outside on his stolen horse looking as innocent as a new born baby, and even stayed put when the other two, came out of the toll house, re-mounted their horses and rode off. Within minutes the angry frightened toll keeper came out of her house and unaware of Abraham's complicity, pleaded for his assistance. Assuring the old lady that he would do all in his power to catch the villains spurred his horse and rode off in pursuit. With the ruse having successfully worked, the three men met up an hour or so later at an inn in Hallatrow, where they took liquid refreshments, paid for of course with their ill-gotten gains. Although the stop was intended to be a celebration of their achievement, with a substantial quantity of alcohol mixing with the adrenalin still pumping through their veins, the three men decided that they had the ability to do more, and accordingly left the inn and rode off towards Paulton. Passing a wayside inn, which had a rather deserted looked about it, the three villains agreed that the opportunity was too good to miss, and dismounted. Leaving one to stand guard and hold the horses, the other two entered the premises, and being careful not to be seen, managed to carry away around £15 worth of goods. (Probably in excess of £6,500 by to-days values) Flushed with success, they burdened the horses with the stolen property, re-mounted and rode off further into the village. However they had not gone very far before they realised that, should they be spotted and a chase ensued, it would be difficult for the over loaded horses to out run the local constabulary nag. Suddenly, Isles noticed that they were passing a small stable, which appeared to be empty apart from a sole occupant who was contentedly munching his way through a bag of hay. With their prayers answered, they soon left the village of Paulton, with the spare horse now carrying the bulk of the stolen goods, plus an extra saddle, which had been purloined from the stables simply because it happened to be there.

Having returned to Bitton and their respective homes, well content with what they had achieved that day, plus the contentment arising from a full stomach and five or six pints of the best local ale, they made room for the retained plunder, and retired to bed, with plans to dispose of the stolen goods during the course of the next few days. Little thought had been given to the possibility that they might have been seen, and recognized, and accordingly it must have come as quite a surprise to Abraham Isles, when he was rudely awakened from his deep slumbers around six o'clock on the Saturday morning, by two or three members of the Bitton constabulary, and arrested on suspicion of theft. A quick search of the house produced all the evidence they needed, with some of the prized booty forming part of the filling of his own pillow, whilst even more incredibly, one of the stolen horses was found in the pantry! Still somewhat dazed by the existence of these unwanted visitors to his abode, Isles put up little resistance, and was unceremoniously bundled away and removed to the Bridewell at Shepton Mallet. At the subsequent Ilchester assizes, Abraham Isles was found guilty of theft, and sentenced to seven years transportation.

Whilst the Bitton constabulary were concentrating on apprehending Isles, Abraham Scull was also in the house, having spent the night in the spare room, but having found that the bed was not as comfortable as his own, he had not slept that well, and had in fact been up and about for almost an hour before the arrival of the constables. Being that more alert, Scull was able to duck out of sight, and make his escape, whilst the constables were upstairs. As far as is known, neither he nor Robert Webb were ever charged with the theft of the horses, and/or the stolen property.

Other similar instances certainly occurred during the eighteenth and well into the nineteenth centuries, and have been used as a background so that two hundred and fifty years or so later we can begin to understand what brought these men to their particular chosen lifestyle.

Into this harsh, uncompromising, difficult world came the Caine family whose problems and set backs were probably no worse or no better than the many other families that inhabited the same world, but who, for reasons which might be found in the above background, decided with other members of their extended family, to turn to petty crime, and to lay down a legacy which would spread their notoriety far and wide as the *COCK ROAD GANG,* and this is their story.

******

Cock Road existed long before it gained notoriety as the generic name given to the so-called gang, and almost certainly it did not adopt that title because of any connection with cock fighting, however tough and lawless the inhabitants might have been, but more than likely obtained its name during the eleventh/twelve centuries from the practice of maintaining narrow pathways along the forest/scrubland floor for the sole purpose of driving birds through the clearing towards nets where they would be caught to supplement the meagre diet. The parish of Oldland, which until the latter part of the nineteenth century extended its boundary as far north as Charnhill, and as far west as Conham, includes a number of place names with connections to birds, such as Cockshot Hill, and Woodstock Hill.

When the Caines' first settled in this part of the world is not known, nor is the precise location of their homes, but if it is your intention to live off your wits at the expense of others, then what better place to choose as a lookout point then the early warning position at the top of the hill, where the approach roads from Bristol or from Chippenham could be seen, thus providing possible warning of any advancing authority. However, such reasoning is purely speculative, and there is no guarantee that any of the Caines actually lived in Cock Road, and it should not be overlooked that during the eighteenth/nineteenth centuries and beyond, Cockroad was the name given to an area larger than a reasonable size village.

Although there is no positive connection with either Cock Road, or any criminal activities, or even any identification as direct antecedents with those who were subsequently found guilty, the earliest record so far discovered of the Caines, is a *WILLIAM KAYNES* who is recorded as the father of *Thomas, Andrew, William* and *Abraham,* all of whom were baptised at St Mary's Bitton on the 19 August 1621, the 28 April 1624, the 4 April 1627 and the 9 September 1631 respectively. Unfortunately, their Mother's name is not given, but it may be reasonable to speculate that *JEANE,* the wife of William Caines, who died in October 1633, was their Mother. If that were the case then it would appear that Jeane also gave birth to a daughter, who was baptised as *Jane* on the 13 June 1633, and who appears to also have died in the same month as her Mother, even though the register has spelt her name Jeane. William Caines then appears to have re-married during 1636, as the next relevant entry is the baptism on the 23 March 1637 of *Mary*, the daughter of William and Mary Caines. William is recorded as having died in July 1662, probably aged around 64 years. His eldest son Thomas fathered, *Samuel* who was baptised on the 21 September 1648, and *Abigail,* who was baptised 11 December 1655.

* * * * *

The first of the Caines to come to any form of criminal prominence was *ABRAHAM CAINES* who was born around 1707. As so often in these matters when investigating unsavoury characters of the past, little if anything is recorded until they are caught even though, in their own surroundings, they became conspicuous many months/years earlier by being that little bit different to the rest of the community. With very few people able to write, and with perhaps many more intimidated by the presence of that particular member of the populace, the activities of the individual and/or his/her family simply became the subject of gossip, which, with the passage of time, will fade from the memory, although some of the story, with parts left out and other parts, which are not necessary the truth, heavily embellished, will ultimately continue through time as a form of folklore. However, as far as Abraham Caines is concerned little if anything is known about him including the identification of his parents, and siblings but, from a statement made at his trial, it is possible to piece together the strong probability that his father, and possibly a number of his uncles were already involved in petty, if not serious crime before Abraham was born. Almost certainly, he and his brothers grew up within a strong criminal fraternity, and were not educated with the three R's, but with the trinity of rules of, do not get caught, have little or no respect for other peoples property, and thirdly do not turn informer or betray your friends.

For hundreds of years, the law allowed individuals to protect themselves, and their family by force if necessary, and particularly in the case of the upper classes, this law also applied to their property. As it was that class which helped to mould and fashion the law, without being encumbered by any form of social conscience and certainly no political correctness, capital punishment was widely used as a deterrent, and a means of keeping the rowdy and uncouth "peasants" subservient to themselves. In addition there was one other important ingredient in this recipe of penal law, which was that those who dished out the punishment were themselves an active part of the upper class, accordingly, many working men and women went to meet their maker dangling at the end of a rope for having committed, by today's standards a paltry misdemeanour that currently would receive little more than a caution, and a pat on the back with the hackneyed phrase "Don't do it again my son"

Abraham and his family almost certainly understood the punishment that could be inflicted upon them should they get caught, but desperation and bravado, mixed no doubt with the over confidence that they would not get caught, pushed them on to steal what they could when they could, and for much of the time they appear to have got away with a life of crime. But ultimately the greed and/or carelessness of a young man's over self-reliance got the better of Abraham during his twentieth year, and he was arrested and charged with theft. Committed to appear at the Gloucester Assizes in 1727, Abraham was found guilty of theft, and sentenced to be hanged at Gloucester Prison. At his trial, when Abraham was of course not represented, it was recorded that he was a member of a gang of thieves, and rogues, some of whom were his brothers. So ended the relatively short life of the first of the Caines to have a known criminal record.

The next Caines to be specifically identified is *BENJAMIN CAINES* who was born around 1728, and who is probably either the son or nephew of the above named Abraham. Like his antecedent, Benjamin Snr. grew up as part of a criminal fraternity, which would not only have included his siblings but also first, and second cousins, with surnames such as Britton, England, Fry and Wilmot, and probably many others. As he grew into manhood he would certainly have observed the lawbreaking that was undoubtedly going on all around him, and the perplexing skills of the various felonious trades would have been watched and then acquired as his dexterity improved. However, crime is not just about the adroitness of the individual concerned, and as there appears to be no record of Benjamin Snr. being charged with any illegal activities during his formative years or afterwards, we must presume that he was either very clever, very lucky or simply did not apply himself to any criminal activities, although the latter would seem to be the most unlikely. It is probably more apt to describe Benjamin Snr. whilst he was growing up as a petty criminal who was not over greedy, and very lucky, which may well have continued when he reached adulthood, but by then he was able to use his skills and knowledge to better effect by organising others to carry out the "dirty-work". All that we can be certain is that no recorded charges were laid before him, and there is no record of him ever having appeared in Court.

Sometime around 1754, Benjamin Snr. married his sweetheart and cousin, *LYDIA BRITTON* at St Mary's Church Bitton, and between them they had at least three sons, *THOMAS, (b1755) BENJAMIN Jnr. (b1757) and RICHARD (b1759),* although there is a very strong probability that they are also the parents of *SAMUEL* who was born circa 1754. Marriage and fatherhood did not however deter Benjamin Snr. from continuing his petty criminal activities, although his luck seemed to stay with him, or more likely he had sufficient bullying sway with the local populace that no one was prepared to point a finger at him for fear of retaliation. However, Benjamin tried his luck once too far, for during 1763 he was charged and convicted of the exceedingly minor crime of illegally selling beer without a licence and fined. This seems to be the sum total of Benjamin's official dally with the eighteenth century criminal justice, as a few years later around 1770, he died, leaving his widow Lydia, free to marry his cousin, *ABRAHAM FRY,* and for her to subsequently give birth to yet another son, who was given the first name *SAMPSON*.

As far as can be reasonably determined Benjamin's eldest son was Samuel, born around 1754. Because our knowledge of these individuals is confined to records, which "highlight" certain moments in their lives, nothing more is known of Samuel until the 14th June 1774 when he married *SUSANNAH HAWKINS* at St. Mary's Bitton. As far as can be determined, this couple had at least three children, *BENJAMIN*, baptised at the same church on the 15th December 1777, *ROBERT* (Baptised 1st June 1783) and *MARY* (Baptised 1st January 1797). Assuming that each was a young child when they were baptised, then there appears to be large time gaps between each birth, which might indicate that the father had been away for long periods of time, either in service of his Country, or in prison. It is of course possible that there may have been other children born to the couple whose records have not been identified, or who may have died at birth or in early infancy, or it is possible that Susannah had difficulty in conceiving, however, in view of the criminal record of the Caines family it is tempting to speculate that he was in prison.

Apart from knowing the date and place of their baptism, nothing more is known of either Robert or Mary, but information has been discovered about their elder brother Benjamin as he has been traced to the surviving Bristol Gaol Delivery Fiats, which are orders issued by the court and signed by the Judge at the time of a court sitting under the king's commission of Assize. In one of these records it shows Benjamin, at the tender age of 12 years, together with nine other defendants, appearing before the sitting Judge on Tuesday 30th March 1790, charged with, and tried on several Indictments for

Felonies. Presumably on this occasion the evidence against them, which may have been collective or individual was insufficient to establish any guilt, and the Judge ordered that they should all be discharged.

Three years later, on the 6th April 1793, Benjamin, once again came before a Judge, this time sitting at the Bristol Lent Assizes, with his co-conspirators *JOSEPH GREEN* and *WILLIAM JEFFERIS* to try and plead mitigation against their earlier sentence. Apparently at the General Quarter Session of Peace held in the City and County of Bristol, on Monday the 14th January 1793, all three had stood in the dock severally charged with Grand Larceny. On this occasion the evidence was good enough for all three to be convicted, and an order was made that *"all three should be transported to such Place or Places Part or Parts beyond the Seas as His Majesty, with the advice of his Privy Council, should declare and appoint for the term of seven years"*. For all of them their appeal fell on stony ground, and the Judge declared that they should remain on the said order. At this stage the three cohorts were almost certainly returned to either the Gloucestershire prison at Lawford's Gate, or the Bristol prison of Newgate, or possibly to a hulk lying off Portsmouth or some other south coastal area, staying there for at least the next twelve months, as on the 12th April 1794 they once again put their case before a Judge sitting at the Bristol Lent Assizes, to plead for mitigation, although the basis of the appeal is not recorded. Once again their petition was turned down, and the order remained in force.

A Calendar of all the prisoners in His Majesty's Gaol of Newgate, in the City and County of Bristol, for felony and other criminal matters, dated the 7th April 1795, shows Joseph, William and Benjamin still held within those walls, and interestingly the same document shows their ages at the date of the trial to be 21; 19 and 15 respectively, identifying this Benjamin to be the son of Samuel and Susannah. Although by now their son would have been a young man of seventeen, the chance that either of them actually had an opportunity of being able to see him at Newgate prison is probably quite remote, apart from the fact that if the presumption is true that Samuel may have himself been in prison, then there was likely to be very few occasions for Benjamin to have received a visit, even from his mother. Sadly it is more than likely that this young boy about to move into adulthood never saw his parents again after he had been arrested back in 1792, especially as it is believed that Benjamin and his friends were shipped out to the colonies sometime later in 1795.

The next in line after Samuel was *THOMAS,* who was born around 1755. Unfortunately that very limited piece of information is as much as we know of Thomas, with the exception that it is believed that he married *ELIZABETH (BETTY) WILLMOTT* at St Mary's Bitton on the 3rd October 1791. Between them, they had around ten children, the first of whom appears to be *MARY* who was probably born in 1800, certainly she was baptised at St Mary's on the 16th August 1800. In total there were seven girls, including *ANN* and *ELIZABETH* who both unfortunately died in early childhood, and twins, who were given their dead sister's names, plus a *SARAH* and a *LUCY*. In addition there were three boys, *ALEXANDER, THOMAS* and *JOSHUA* of whom Thomas was the eldest of that trio. Sometime around 1815 Thomas fathered an illegitimate son who, as *GEORGE PEACOCK,* took on his mother's maiden name, possibly on the grounds that his father's name could be a rather dangerous possession especially if at anytime George came up before the law. However, retaining his mother's surname did not protect him, and George became yet another grandson of Benjamin and Lydia to be transported.

After Thomas came Benjamin Jnr. who also has left little if any documentary evidence of his life, with the only known facts being he was born around 1757, and that during 1777, he married his childhood sweetheart, *ANN COOL,* at St Mary the Virgin, Bitton and between them they appear to have had at least ten children, although it would seem that it was only seven of them whose activities actually perpetuated the Cock Road Gang myth.

Later in life, and some eight years after Benjamin, his younger brother *RICHARD* was born. Like all who went before him little if anything is known about his early years, how he grew up and what type of person he was. It seems inconceivable that Richard's upbringing would have been any different to that of his brothers, but for one reason or another, Richard chose not to go down the path of criminal activity, or to put it another way, he does not appear to have ever been caught. Instead, history has recorded that he was a gardener by trade, and that having been baptised at St. Mary's Bitton at the advanced age of seventeen years, he courted and subsequently married *HANNAH NICHOL* in the same church on the 27th June 1791. On the Register, he is shown as a bachelor of this parish, whilst Hannah is described as a spinster from St. George. Between them they had at least five children, *SAMUEL* born August 1794; *RICHARD* born 1795; *THOMAS* born 1797; *MARY* born 1808, and *SARAH* born 1810

THE CHILDREN OF BENJAMIN and ANN

Their first child, who was born in 1778, was a son to whom they gave the name *GEORGE,* and he was soon indoctrinated into the ways of the family and grew up with a limited degree of formal education, although by the time that he had reached his teens he was well educated in the ways of living outside of the law in what continued to be a very tough and ruthless environment. Like his father and grandfather before him he avoided falling foul of the magistrates and local constabulary, either by luck, by wit or by reputation, although it is possible that his parents ensured that their prodigy was kept sufficiently far in the background as to allow others to pay for the crimes of the "family business". However, unlike those who went before him, George had his own ideas and ambitions to spread his wings, and seek out new areas to plunder. By his late teens, George had begun to spread his wings, and in conjunction with his cousins, particularly *FRANK BRITTON,* he frequented fairs and gatherings, well away from his home, where their faces were less recognisable, and where, as a consequence, they could steal or swindle the honest, and sometimes the not so honest citizen from his or her money. Occasionally they would ride into Bristol, but that city was a little too close to home, and there was always the risk of being seen by someone from Kingswood and/or the surrounding districts, who might bear a grudge, and who would happily denounce the pair, even if it was anonymously. More often than not they would strike north to the cities of Gloucester and/or Cheltenham, and living off their acumen and ability to steal, they would stay away from home for weeks on end, roaming the countryside from one fair to another. Quite frequently their wanderings would take them over the border into Wales, but even that area subsequently proved to be unsafe. Almost certainly, George did not have the finesse or caution of his forefathers and no doubt pumped up with the enthusiasm of youth, he threw caution to the wind and decided that a very good way of making money, without the involvement of any hard laborious physical effort was to handle counterfeit coinage. Whether either George or Francis (Frank) manufactured the illegal coins, or simply acted as the go between has not been established, but just prior to George's 21st birthday, he and his cousin were arrested at Pontypool for being involved in an altercation with one of the local publicans, and upon being searched for weapons, both men were found to be in possession of a number of forged guineas, as well as a well-mounted horse, which was subsequently identified as having been stolen. The cousins were then charged with passing counterfeit coins, and were sent for trial at Monmouth to appear before the sitting of the 1799 Lent Quarter Assize Courts. With the evidence of the guineas in their possession, and the fact that some of the fair traders, with whom they had had dealings, prepared to testify against them, the outcome was a forgone conclusion, and having been found guilty they received the relatively mild sentence of one years imprisonment. That is not to say that eighteenth century imprisonment was easy by any means, but almost certainly had they been found guilty of passing the forged coinage amongst the gentry, then their sentence would have been for a much longer period, or even they may have been transported. At their trial, it was claimed by the prosecution that:

"they belonged to a gang who frequented country fairs as hawkers and pedlars".

However, although it would, in the circumstances of their birth, be quite understandable to presume that the prosecutor was referring to the Caine family and the Cock Road Gang, it is possible that George may have had sufficient independence or desire to operate away from his family which could mean that the "gang" was in fact one that was directly connected with the counterfeit coinage. The manufacture of the illegal coins would almost certainly have required a considerable amount of effort, skill and financial wealth, so that a suitable foundry could be set up, without drawing too much attention to itself, and for the labourers and the forger to be given a big enough incentive to remain quiet. In addition there would be raw materials to purchase, plus the need to have a distribution network, which was independent of each other, and which if discovered, would not automatically allow the authorities to trace the coins back to their source of production. To have just two uneducated, if well suited, men peddling the coins around as many markets as they could attend would not have been the best arrangement for those who were masterminding the whole thing, and thus it is quite feasible that there were others besides George and Francis who would have been involved as front men flooding the area with the spurious coins so that their exchange for legitimate coin of the realm could be as large as possible in the shortest conceivable time. As such their undertakings may well have come to the attention of the local constables, and/or magistrates, and whether they were acting either in pairs or as individuals, their activities may easily have been seen as a group of like minded persons, which could quite effortlessly and understandably been identified or seen as gang by the upper classes.

There is, unfortunately, no record of how well or how badly either of the cousins coped with the lack of freedom, but whilst they certainly understood the risks that they were taking, during their gallivanting around the countryside, it is most likely that the confidence of youth probably led them to believe that they would be immune to such punishment, and thus when they entered the prison gates they doubtlessly had little or no idea of the realities of the penal system, and the overwhelming effects of being confined. The one thing which is certain is, that their harsh and rugged background stood them in good stead, as they took their punishment, and came out twelve months later even more determined to live a life of crime, and to get back at authority and the upper classes.

It was not long after George and Francis returned from their enforced sojourn in Monmouthshire, to their native haunts that the pair, together with other relatives, some of whom were more distant than others, began to refresh their skills by relieving many of their fellow inhabitants of Oldland and the surrounding parishes, of their money, goods and chattels, although it must be said that those same inhabitants had, at the time, no real wish to be parted from their possessions. In those not infrequent occasions when the owners were less than willing to hand over their money, goods or chattels, just simply because they had been menacingly asked, they found that George and his relatives were only too happy to try and dissuade them, both verbally and physically, from that particular course of action. The uncomplicated reputation of the family name, very often did the trick, but if that did not work then the threats became more intimidating with weapons being produced and lives were put at risk. Over the next eighteen months or so George, and his fellow cohorts were able to live quite comfortably off the wealth of the local gentry, and no doubt as the cousins would frequently be seen together, the idea that they were a gang was an obvious assumption to make, but whether it was ever an organised gang, with a leader is difficult to judge as of course non of the participants kept any records. Loyalty was very obviously high on the agenda of the group, and it was loyalty, or perhaps more truthfully misplaced loyalty that ultimately led to George's downfall.

During the summer of 1812 *ISAAC COX,* (alias Lewis) who may well have been one of the "gang", but was certainly a long time friend of George, found himself in trouble with the law in the form of *BENJAMIN CURTIS* the local constable, who had just charged Cox with theft and had placed him under arrest. This was no doubt either a very brave, or a very foolhardy thing to do, because Benjamin Curtis was not only on his own, he was also some way from the local magistrate, and somewhere he could incarcerate his prisoner. Word of the arrest soon spread around the community, and certainly George was either on hand or very close to the place of the arrest, as shortly afterwards, and whilst Isaac was putting up a stiff resistance to his particular indignity George arrived. Without any hesitation, George joined the melee having first of all drawn his gun, he fired as his ran towards the constable and missed. With no time to reload he then began using the butt end as a club to beat the constable about the head. Benjamin Curtis was obviously made of sterner stuff, as he stood up against both men, and possibly with the assistance of one or more bystanders, he successfully fought off the villains. Although battered and bruised, Benjamin was able to safely return home and after a short period of recuperation he was back on his feet determined to bring both men to account, particularly George Caines, who by his actions, was now to be charged with attempted murder. It is probably true that if Curtis had been anyone other than the local constable the charge of attempted murder would not have been raised, but here was someone who needed to be protected by the law as he carried out his lawful duties, and there was no way that the local magistrates were going to allow Caines to "get away with it".

In addition, before George even appeared before the magistrates, there was yet another event, which took place in Oldland that, had the unfortunate effect of putting a further nail in his coffin. Apparently, *JAMES FRANCIS,* who was due to give evidence against George in respect of a separate matter, was disturbed during the night by shots, and upon investigation, found that no less than three lead balls had been fired into his house, going through the window and into the bedroom where his three young children had been sleeping. Although fortunately no one was hurt, and although the culprit[s] was never found, the incident did George no good whatsoever, and did not stop James from testifying.

George had little, if any, defence to offer at his subsequent trial, which was held at the Gloucester Assizes, and not unexpectedly, was found guilty of the attempt to unlawfully kill constable Curtis and was sentenced to be hung from the neck until dead. Somewhat surprisingly, and no doubt at great relief to twenty-three year old George, the death sentence was subsequently commuted to transportation for life; he would of course never be able to return home but at least he was alive. For the next two and a half years, George Caines was confined to a stinking, rotting hulk in one of the estuaries along the south coast of England, whilst he awaited an uncertain passage to the other side of the world. Exercise would have been virtually non-existent; food would have been very meagre, extremely unappetising, and maggot infested, whilst in the dense damp interior of the ship, the inmates would have been riddled with lice, covered with sores and threatened with the many diseases caused by lack of basic hygiene and humanity being packed together. However, in April 1815, George left the hellhole of the hulk, for the slight improvement of a three or four-month sea journey on the good ship *Fanny* bound for New South Wales. If nothing else, George was a born survivor, as he reached the penal colony and served his time, which subsequently enabled him to receive his freedom in Australia and start a new life. At one time for a number of years he traded as a butcher in Castlereagh Street, Sydney, but eventually he opened a public house in Parramatta, giving it the title *The Jolly Sailor*, possibly after his experience of the journey from England, but romantically it is more likely to have been named after the pub of the same name in Hanham.

* * * * *

The next in line was *FRANCIS CAINES* who was born around 1779 and who like his brother was brought up in the family tradition and ways of crime. As he grew into manhood, his petty crimes increased and changed to more serious misdemeanours with greater risks and greater rewards, although like the majority of his relatives he appears to have avoided a face to face with the Assize Courts, as there do not seem to be any records of criminal charges and/or arrests against him. However, much was to change in July 1804 when four men were taken into custody in the city of Bath, having been charged with the theft of more than £400 worth of fine cloth from premises at Freshford. [probably equivalent to around £86,500 by today's reckoning] Three of the four men were all identified as coming from the Bitton area of Gloucestershire, and were named on the charge sheet as *THOMAS BATT, CHARLES FULLER,* who also used the alias *"The Squire"* because of the airs and graces he gave himself, and Francis Caines, the second son of Benjamin and Ann Caines, with the gaol calendar describing him as being a 23 year old oyster and cider seller. ~~ It should be remembered that during this part of our history, oysters were a cheap form of supplementary diet, being extremely plentiful and not considered the expensive delicacy they are today. Cider was also an inexpensive drink so the only real doubt created by this description is how far did Francis have to go to obtain the oysters, and perhaps more importantly how fresh were they when he sold them? ~~ According to the details that emerged during the trial, the quartet made quite a night of their illicit activities, having first decided to walk to Bath during the early summer's evening, they planned to arrive at an agreed hostelry prior to sunset where they proposed, and in fact had, an enjoyable late supper, of cold mutton, bread and cheese, which was supplemented by an adequate supply of alcohol. Having satisfied their taste buds they left the inn at around 10.00pm and began to make their way on foot to Bathwick; once there they found a suitable stable to break in to and upon gaining entrance, they succeeded in harnessing a large horse to an equally large cart, and removed both from the premises without apparently at anytime disturbing the owner. Tired of walking the four men then drove the cart to Freshford, arriving in that village a little after mid-night. This was not the first time that the four men had been to Freshford, having already been there on two or three separate occasions to seek out and observe the actions of a particular business man who owned a warehouse in the village where large amounts of expensive cloth were stored. It was noted by them that there was a frequent movement of textiles on almost a daily basis, and that a fair amount of cloth was at anyone time left on the premises, which were left unattended at night, although the building was of course locked. With all of the honest villagers fast asleep in their beds, the four men used the strength of the horse and the weight of the cart to smash down the large, if not over secure loading area door, and made their way in to the warehouse, where they loaded as many rolls/bundles of cloth onto the cart as they could in the time allowed them, bearing in mind that many of those sleeping villages had been awoken by the noise created by one of the first forms of naïve "ram-raids", and were beginning to investigate the cause of the pandemonium. However, by the time that those who had got out of bed, wiped the sleep from their eyes and had reached the street, the four men, one spooked horse, and a damaged cart with contents had disappeared into the blackness of the night, and no one had the desire to follow what was undoubtedly a very large gang of ruffians.

As part of what was, quite definitely, an elaborate plan, Charles Fuller had a week or so previously visited Bath, and using a pseudonym, had rented for a month, a coach house just off Pultney Street. Thus having pushed the horse as fast as it would go over hill and dale, the foursome entered the city of Bath around one-thirty in the morning and drove to the coach house where, hopefully unseen, they unloaded the cart, which they left inside the coach house and secreted the fabric in the hay loft, having already given water and hay to the sweating and heavily breathing horse. Content in the belief if not knowledge that they had done all that they could to make adequate plans for the theft, and to have covered up their movements, the four men made their way home through the deserted streets of Bath, and over the Kelston hills and on to Bitton.

Probably, with the benefit of hindsight, the plan was not that well drawn up and doubtlessly all four had attempted a robbery that was more than they could handle. As far as can be determined, they had no specific plans and/or arrangements to dispose of the cloth, which after all would not be the most easiest of items to exchange for money especially in a non specialist market, and the nature of the textiles were such that only the upper class and well-off would have had sufficient money to purchase and use the stolen cloth. For the average family living in and around Oldland at the time, the existence of such fine cloth would have been an embarrassment but even more particularly, the cloth would have been virtually useless to them in their harsh environment. In addition the quartet do not seem to have appreciated that the pattern of the cloth would make it extremely identifiable, nor do they seem to have taken into consideration the resulting hue and cry, particularly from the wealthy, that they would have caused by their audacious raid.

Although it may have been assumed by all four of them, that by carrying out such a raid under the cover of darkness it would somehow give them complete anonymity, they completely overlooked the fact that inevitably there is always someone around to see what is happening and to put two and two together. Additionally, as already mentioned, the easy part was the theft, the difficult part was disposing of the cloth for money, bearing in mind that they had already incurred the cost of renting the coach house, there was the additional fact that they needed to divide the spoils between all four, some of whom were less patient than others. However, there was even one further problem that they do not appear to have considered during the planning stage, which could quite easily have been, and possible was their Achilles heel, and that was how to dispose of the large horse, currently eating its way through most of the hay in the coach house, and how to dispose of the equally large and somewhat damaged cart. Even if the cart was not so easily identifiable, and it probably was, the true owner of the horse would undoubtedly soon recognize his equine servant roaming the streets. Neither were easy things to hide, and neither were easy things to throw away, there was of course another two or three weeks left on the short term rent of the coach house, but the horse would need feeding, and that would cost money, and as the cloth was not being converted into money there was an unconsidered problem that was to prove to be a fatal flaw in their plans.

During the early part of the nineteenth century, theft was regarded as a very serious crime, although in reality, the gravity of the felony was scaled to the individual wealth of the victim. If you were a pauper then the level of seriousness was probably down to it having been you own fault, on the other hand, if you had money and influence then the crime was so grave as to attract a capital punishment penalty. The victim chosen by the gang of four was wealthy and had a lot of influence, and this crime against his property was not going to go unpunished, as the streets of Bath rang with rumour and counter-rumour, all hoping that a reward would be paid by the warehouse owner, should the criminal be found and his property recovered. Such was the hue and cry that it was only a matter of days after the theft had taken place arrests were starting to be made, and in less than two weeks, part of the gang were in custody at Ilchester Gaol, however, for reasons which have now been lost in time, only Francis was actually charged with the theft of the cloth.

With lawyers unwilling to risk their reputation, let alone their fee on defending these unsophisticated criminals, Francis Caines decided that the most honourable thing he could do was to plead guilty by confessing his part in the theft, without in anyway incriminating any of the others. Yes it was true that he had stolen a horse, and yes he had also stolen a cart taking both away without the consent of the owner. It was also true that he had broken into the warehouse at

Freshford, and yes he had stolen a quantity of fine cloth but, and this point was critical in Francis' mind for mitigation to be considered, no one had been physically hurt, and most of the cloth, and the horse and cart had been returned to their rightful owners. Surely a reasonable set of circumstances that any right-minded person would have take into deliberation before considering meting out the punishment. However, we are dealing with the magistrates at Ilchester who were in no mood to give these matters any such attention, for as far as they were concerned, the prisoner standing before them had violated and assaulted the victims, victims that were after all from their own class. Just by his sheer audacity alone to have consider stealing from them, let alone to have actually carried out the dastardly deed, meant that the prisoner was simply not entitled to any form of mitigation, and further more, it was extremely impertinent of him that he should even have contemplated that they may have considered any form of extenuating circumstances. Men like you, they pontificated, cannot expect to get away with stealing from the rich; you are the scum of the earth and as such can expect no mercy from this Court. Accordingly, Francis was sentenced by the Court to be hung, by the neck, until dead, as an example to those who should dare attack members of the establishment. With the execution-taking place at Ilchester Gaol during September 1804 Francis, at the tender age of 25 became the first of the Caines to receive the ultimate punishment for his life of crime.

Just a short thirteen months previously, Francis had stood in front of the altar at St. Mary's Bitton with his young bride *ELIZABETH STEPHENS* on his arm, and now as he swung at the end of a rope, Elizabeth was either pregnant with their son, or had not long before given birth, so whether Francis ever saw his son also named Francis will never be known, and no doubt emotions ran high when a year later, baby Francis was christened in the same church where his parents had married.

Whether his young bride, or any of his relatives managed to see and say good bye to him at Ilchester, or whether any were at his execution is not known, but certainly a week or so after his death, the family arranged for his body to be recovered and brought back to Oldland. Once back amongst his own kind, Francis was washed and cleaned and placed in a better quality coffin for subsequent burial at St. Mary's Bitton, the very same church that twenty-seven year's previously his parents had stood together as they made their marriage vows. Sitting across the churchyard wall, whilst the female relatives wept, as the coffin was lowered in to the ground, was Francis' eleven-year old brother, Benjamin, who persisted in blowing a tuneless whistle throughout the whole proceedings, little did he know that it would not be that long before he himself would join his brother.

* * * * *

Having had two sons during the first three years of their married life, in 1781 the union between Benjamin and Ann was blessed with a daughter whom they christened *ELIZABETH* but who was known throughout her life as *BETTY*. As with her elder siblings, Betty grew up amidst the petty crime of her parents, aunts, and uncles, and other members of her extended family, and no doubt dabbled in such events herself. Like her brothers, there appears to be no criminal record against her, certainly during her formative years, all that can be ascertained is that by the end of her teenage years she had become adamant that marriage, or more particularly the marriage service was not for her, and that she was comfortable with all of the crime that surrounded her. By the time she was twenty-three, Betty had begun to live, as husband and wife, with a *TIMOTHY BUSH* the son of a local coalmining family, and in 1805 presented him with a son whom they called *JAMES* with the surname Caines being prominent, although in later life he would occasionally use the alias Bush. Two years later a second son was born to the couple, and in memory of his late uncle was given the name *FRANCIS*. Whether Timothy had any leanings towards petty or even more serious crime when he first met Betty will never be known for certain, but it is probably reasonable to presume that living in such a small and insular community, it would be almost impossible for Timothy not to have known about Betty's background and the type of family she was from, and that accordingly he was likely to have had many sympathies with such a life style, and may even have hankered after such a life style himself. Certainly as the years with Betty rolled by he must have come across her own sympathies and occasional shady dealings and in particular her desire to help wherever possible her brothers in their illegal activities. On one occasion, around 1810, Timothy came home to find a small herd of pigs happily mucking about in the front parlour, whilst Betty went about her chores. Apparently, her brother George together with *ISAAC CRIBB* and *GEORGE HATHAWAY* his friends and local characters, plus Isaac Cox had, on the spur of the moment, stolen these pigs and, having driven them away from their owner's property suddenly realised that they had nowhere to hide the animals until they could be disposed of. Whether Betty offered, or brother George asked will now never be known, but there they were occupying the front parlour, normally kept for important guests.

Whatever was felt or known by Timothy as he entered into his relationship with Betty will have to remain a secret but the inevitability of taking such action meant that sooner or later he would become embroiled, as shown above, in the criminal activities of Betty's family. One thing that will have surely occurred to him, during those early days of the relationship was that without doubt, it was much easier to obtain money through the illegal means employed by her family, than the pittance he could earn grafting underground for someone else to make a profit. The problem of course with crime is that if you are unlucky you are caught, but that was a risk worth taking, after all there were greater risks working as a coalminer. Accordingly, Timothy embarked on his life of crime trying to learn as much as he could from Betty's family, whilst at the same time trying to remain as independent as he could, and thus wherever possible, Timothy would either work alone, or with Betty's cousins rather than her brothers. However, Timothy did not have the skill or the necessary luck of his non in-law brothers as, after enjoying a relatively short life of transgressions he fell foul of the law whilst in company with *THOMAS WILMOT* and an eighteen-year-old *JOSEPH WILLIS,* when they were charged during 1810 with the heinous crime of horse stealing. Such a theft was regarded at that time as a very major invasion into the deeply held privileges of the rich, and accordingly for anyone caught and found guilty the crime carried the death penalty. With little or no mitigating circumstances to defend themselves with at the Gloucestershire Assizes, the trio resorted to trying to claim that they were nowhere near the stables at the time that the horses were stolen, and that there was the matter of miss identity. Not surprisingly, all three were found guilty and condemned to death. This was the basic sentence nearly always given at the end of such trials, but more often than not, the death penalty was commuted to transportation, and with providence smiling upon them, a day or so after the hearing, they were each told that they would not be hanged but that instead they would be sent to the antipodes on a single ticket. Accordingly, on the 26th August 1813, Timothy Bush, together with his compatriots, Thomas Wilmot, and Joseph Willis, sailed from these shores onboard the sailing vessel *General Hewart,* bound for New South Wales, and the start of a new, if somewhat arduous life as a convict, in the full and certain knowledge that he was never likely to see either Betty, or their two sons again.

With two young sons to bring up, and to all intents and purposes, her partner dead, the very resourceful Betty lost no time in forging a new relationship and probably long before the *General Hewart* reached the coast of New South Wales, she had opened her door to twenty-four year old *GEORGE GROVES,* presenting him with a son *THOMAS CAINES (alias Groves)* during 1814. George already had a reputation for being a petty thief, and had previously been in trouble with the Law. For example, during 1808, the seventeen-year-old George Groves had been arrested and charged with stealing a quantity of leather breeches and other articles of clothing from William Snellgrove of Keynsham. At his arrest, some of the items were found in his possession, whilst other items of clothing were subsequently found at the home of his parents in Bitton. At his trial, in December 1808, George was found guilty, but as he had only stolen from an artisan his punishment was scaled down to six months hard labour at the Lawford's Gate House of Correction. Undeterred by the experience of the sentence, upon being released George quickly resumed his illegal activities as in June 1809, whilst legitimately selling gingerbread at the Chepstow Wool Fair, he was arrested for having tried to supplement his earnings with a little pick-pocketing on the side. The sentence he received probably consisted of a further period of hard labour, but the exact details are not known. At this point, George seems to disappear, as nothing is recorded of him until he moved in with thirty-three year old Betty.

As far as is known, Betty had no other pregnancies, and appears to have lived quite happily with George for the next seven years or so.

As for George, he was again in trouble with the Law during 1815 although, exactly what for has not been determined, all that appears to have been noted during the period he was in custody is that he was described as the leader of a notorious gang. Once again in the documents there is a mention of a gang, but as on other occasions, no description is given to the so-called gang, and no names are included with the reference. It would seem unlikely that he would have been in charge of the Cock Road Gang, if such a gang existed, unless the Caines acted as some form of benevolent "godfather" and allowed their young protégée to take over the reigns from time to time. More likely, George was probably seen in the company of other villains and that that group may well have been perceived by those who may have been intimidated by it, or seen by the local constabulary as a gang.

In general, George seems to have fitted in quite well with Betty and her ready-made brood, with both James and Francis accepting their new "Dad" and their new brother without any apparent difficulties, or certainly none that have come to light. Apart from taking on the mantle of Father to three growing lads, George also began to adopt the ways of Betty's wider relations, and became more and more involved in petty crime as a way of augmenting his gingerbread income to meet the ever increasing needs of raising a family. In addition he was also keen to pass on to the boys, the skills and knowledge of his adopted family, although all of this was about to be cut short, but not before he had adopted the style "Captain"

For the next four years or so, George managed to hone his skill of pick pocketing, whilst at the same time keeping one step ahead of the law. However, in August 1820 at Lansdown Fair, he was seen by a constable surreptitiously removing an article from someone else's coat, and was immediately apprehended. Fairs such as the one at

Lansdown, attracted many would-be pickpockets, and in August 1820, there were sufficient freebooters to successfully organise a rescue, and George was set free and allowed to disappear amongst the crowd. Such was his reputation, the *Gloucester Journal* reported on the 4th September 1820, that the:

"Bristol Fair commenced on Friday and it was quickly noticed that the light-fingered corps had a strong detachment there, however there was a notable absentee, Captain Groves who is apparently away on the sick list. We wish we could add that rather than being unwell he was just sick of his trade."

We shall never know whether "Captain" George Groves ever read the article himself, but the insult did not put him off, in fact he probably revelled in the notoriety, although such fame did not help him with his pick pocketing skills, and as a consequence he spread his wings and visited fairs well away from Gloucestershire and Somersetshire.

It was during January 1822 when George was next arrested and charged with the theft of watches. Held in custody until he appeared before the magistrates in Derby, George was found guilty once too often, and with little sympathy coming from the judge in the Midlands, he was sentenced to be transported to New South Wales for a term of seven years, although with little chance of being able to earn enough money once he was free, to pay for a passage home, the sentence might just as well read for life.

It has been said above that Betty was very much against the institution of marriage, and certainly put her forthright views into practice. However, whilst she may have either directly or indirectly brought about much of her own family's adversity upon herself, although it might be said that the die was cast the moment she was born a Caines, sympathy must surely be given to Elizabeth for the many losses which occurred in a relatively short span of time. By 1840, when she was 59 years of age, she had experienced the loss of one son, to the hangman's noose, plus two common-law husbands, and two other sons, forced to depart these shores for good. If that record is not bad enough, Betty also had the pain of having two brothers executed, and two more transported. Thus to have three male relatives hung, and six transported, all in the space of twenty-one short years, is either down to extreme bad luck, or gross negligence, and may well create a record which would be unenvied by all.

Fortunately this is not the end of Betty's story, as albeit the emotional pain and anguish presumably remained with her, as time past the ache in her heart diminished, and was replaced with the love of the new man in her life, *JOSEPH WILLIS*. Either through his influence, or Betty's mellowing with age, her long held views on marriage diminished, and in 1841 at the age of sixty, she married labourer, Joseph Willis at Holy Trinity Church, Kingswood. A copy of their marriage certificate reveals that he was over full age, the son of Joseph, a lime burner, whilst Elizabeth's father Benjamin is described, for the first time in the written records as a greengrocer, thus, perhaps he had also mellowed with age, and the loss of his children. The certificate shows that neither Joseph, nor Elizabeth could read or write. As a side issue it is perhaps interesting to speculate that Betty's husband is the same Joseph Willis who was transported to Australia together with her first partner Timothy Bush. However, as both men received a life sentence, it is unlikely that that Joseph Willis ever returned to these shores. Alternatively, Joseph, friend of Timothy, had a son also called Joseph and thus it is possible that Betty married Joseph Jnr., who would have been some twenty years or so younger than her. Of course it is just as possible that the name is a coincident and is not related to either of these men, but whatever was the connection, let us hope in the circumstances, that they had a happy life together.

* * * * *

After Elizabeth, was born in 1781, there appears to have been a gap of some five years before the next child arrived but it is believed that Ann had at least one other baby during that time but that unfortunately the child did not survive. Apart from the five year gap, the evidence for making this assumption is the fact that recorded in the Bitton Register on the 19th December 1784 are four baptisms, for George, Francis, Elizabeth and Benjamin, all children of Benjamin and Ann Caines, and all having taken place on that day. George would have course been seven years old, Francis around five years, and their sister three years, but why wait that long, and why have them all baptised together in December 1784. One answer could be that when the youngest child was born he may have been unwell, and had not long to live, bearing in mind that child mortality at this time was extremely high. Alternatively he may have survived his first few months only to succumb to a winter ailment, whatever the reason, (assuming there is one) it was perhaps such a situation that acted as the catalyst for Benjamin and Ann deciding that now was the time to bring the children to church, as they did not want baby Benjamin to die and end up in purgatory.

The one thing, which is certain is that, as the Benjamin, for whom we have details, was not born until 1793 he cannot be the Benjamin, baptised on The 19th December 1784. It should also be remembered that unlike today, our forefathers thought nothing of giving a new child the same name as a deceased sibling, and with Benjamin Snr. almost certainly desirous to have his name carried through to the next generation, he would have had no hesitation in giving his name to another son.

* * * * *

Thus the next surviving child would appear to be Thomas who was born in 1786 and almost certainly he too grew up with a limited amount of education as far as the three R's were concerned, but plenty of tuition in the ways of crime. By the time he reached his teenage years Thomas had two older brothers one of whom was already serving a prison sentence, and one who was gaining amongst the criminal world a reputation as a daring if not reckless individual, and there was nothing more than young Thomas wanted but to emanate and join his brothers, and earn his own reputation, not realising that before he graduated into manhood, one of those brothers would be dancing at the end of the hangman's rope.

Despite his brother's death, Thomas was keen, impulsive and naïve to get going, and soon joined the fray and was organising, without necessarily a great deal of thought, a number of burglaries and theft, although for the most part they were relatively minor crimes, and there were no resulting arrests. As the years rolled by, and Thomas honed his skills as he tried at first to follow in his eldest brother's footsteps, and then tried to become more independent and important in his own right, however, he still watched and admired his brother, but developed his own traits, which included a leaning to the theatrical aspect of being more of a showman. All of course was to change during 1814 when George was arrested, and subsequently sentenced to be transported for life, as Thomas was now the eldest brother living in Oldland and as such felt that his new position in the hierarchy of the close knit society in which he lived, plus his hard won reputation was lacking something, and accordingly decided that he would give himself the exulted title of "Captain Tom", despite the fact that it is difficult to understand exactly what he thought he was captain of, unless he saw his compatriots as a gang.

One of the important factors that always helped to bind brothers, cousins, and friends together in a loose form of affinity was loyalty, as already displayed by George when he unwisely attacked

Benjamin Curtis. Perhaps such acts were simply based upon bravado or the need to impress that they had the courage, tenacity and mob rule right to be the leader, the top man, or the person in charge. With one of his two elder brothers already dead as a result of the hangman's skill, and the other brother on his way to the antipodes, with a one-way ticket, Thomas Caines had to prove himself, especially as he had by now given himself the title of Captain. Such an opportunity presented itself when, around May 1815, Isaac Cribb, a fish carrier by trade, and a known associate of brother George, was apprehended and placed in the lock-up on the main street at Bitton. If for no other reason than to get back at the legal system for their treatment of his brothers, "Captain Tom" felt a strong urge to do something about the injustice of locking up poor Isaac Cribb, and decided that he could lead a band of friends to the prison and affect a rescue.

Like so many things undertaken by the Caines and their associates, they allowed their passion to rule their head, and acted on impulse with little if any thought for the consequences of their action, or of their own safety. Such was the situation on this occasion as, having gathered together his younger brother Benjamin, and a number of their joint friends, some of whom were armed with clubs and sticks, Captain Tom led this band of ruffians through the main street of Bitton, with the intention of making a frontal attack on the lock-up, which was situated some 10 feet above the level of the road, well constructed of stone, and contained two very determined constables, who had already been tipped off that an attempt to release Isaac Cribb was likely to be attempted and accordingly had sent for reinforcements. Having barricaded themselves in, and ensured that Mr. Cribb was sufficiently restrained and could cause them no trouble, constables *MOSES BATT* and *CHARLES BULL* were well prepared to resist the taunts and brickbats hurled at them, most of which fell like water on a ducks back. By now, the disturbance had caused a number of onlookers to arrive, many of whom were urchins and wasters, but they were all prepared to offer Captain Tom advice, and to throw their own taunts at whichever group seemed to be losing the battle. In reality, Thomas Caines and his friends never had a chance of getting in to the lock-up, let alone releasing Isaac Cribb, and it would have been much better if they had all decided to have packed-up and gone home, but commonsense rarely gets in the way of stupidity, so the brickbats continued to be hurled, whilst Caines and one or two others tried to attack the door, completely unaware that a mounted posse of Bristol's constabulary had already reached, and passed the Queen's Head Inn at Willsbridge. Within a matter of minutes, the mounted police were in Bitton and soon, with swords drawn, they were amongst the men attacking the prison, and in less than half and hour, a number of the raiders had been arrested, including Captain Tom himself, and his brother Benjamin.

All of those arrested spent at least one night in prison, although in the following morning they were released without charge. As the main ringleader, Thomas, together with two or three others were held for trial, charged with disturbing the peace, and attempted illegal release of a prisoner and, having been found guilty received a custodial sentence of two years. Thus Thomas's first real attempt to assert his authority, and to stamp his mark on the criminal fraternity, ended in abject failure, and gave him the opportunity of discovering for himself at firsthand, the nature and quality of gaol life in the early nineteenth century. As for Benjamin, he was acquitted, and now became the eldest male Caines available to "run the show".

Such was the reputation of the criminal element in and around Bitton that the story was reported in *Felix Farley's Bristol Journal,* with the comment that the peaceful inhabitants of Bitton and the surrounding area could, as a result of the imprisonment of these *Banditti* :-

"Be divested of many of its terrors, and that those same individuals can now sleep safely in their beds"

But what of Isaac Cribb, who was safely still locked away when law and order had returned to the main street of Bitton. There he remained for the next few weeks, before being taken to Gloucester prison where he awaited his subsequent trial and conviction. Found guilty he was sentenced, to be transported for life, and was sent to a rotting stinking hulk anchored in one of the many creeks that form Portsmouth harbour, to await a suitable passage to the other side of the world. Some time during 1816, he managed to break out of the hulk, get ashore and disappear into the Hampshire countryside. Exactly how long this period of freedom lasted is not known, but three years later in 1819, left these shores for ever, bound for a totally new world "Down-Under".

With the three eldest Caines boys either dead or incarcerated, and Benjamin not quite ready to take over from where brother Thomas had left-off, the level of crime during 1815/16 in and around the Bitton/Oldland Common area diminished somewhat, which led to some of the more honest burghers to take the opportunity to further consider the state of their economy and the anarchy which had surrounded, pestered and infiltrated their lives over many years. Some four years previously, at a meeting of the more prominent members of the community, they had all agreed to form the Kingswood Association for the suppression of thieves, which in practice was little more than a vigilante group prepared to root out at any cost, those whom they considered were villains and general wrongdoers. However with some of the organizers being either magistrates themselves, or having close links with local magistrates, the Association was warned that such action could and almost certainly would break the law, and whilst there was a general air of tacit approval, officially the magistrates could not support anything the Association did that broke the law. Despite this warning, the more hardened and forceful members of the group decided to push ahead with the original concept and to give weight to their intentions they arranged for a "mounted military" arm of the Association to be formed, giving it the style of *The Bitton Cavalry* a group of local land/horse owners who would ride around the countryside, under the authority of *THOMAS BEVAN* equipped with swords, and firearms. Once this mounted group was formed, Thomas Bevan decided that he would emulate Thomas Caines, and give himself the rank of Captain, although as the troop were not officially part of the militia and/or the military in any way, he had no legal right to such title. No doubt allowing his newly acquired position to go to his head, the cavalry trotted around the country lanes with Captain Thomas Bevan in front, trying to look as important as his diminutive stature would allow, and in doing so he and his troopers managed to round up a few urchins, and petty thieves, a number of drunks, and hooligans but little else, and certainly no one who might have been regarded as an important criminal. However, statistically, from 1811/12, the number of offenders committed to prison from the Bitton/Oldland Common area began to increase, with new names occurring in the Gaol Register, although there continued to be a core of the more familiar names.

Quite separate to the efforts of the above, in January 1809, *SAMPSON FRY*, the half brother of Thomas was, together with *SAMUEL COOKE*, also of Bitton, sentenced to jail for one month, having been found guilty of common assault. Four months later during the month of May, *WILLIAM BRYANT* who was aged nineteen, and his seventeen-year-old brother *SAMUEL,* cousins of the Caines, were charged with having broken into *WILLIAM BATMAN'S* house in Bitton, and stolen a quantity of linen, silver buckles, and other articles, for which they received a custodial sentence.

The experience of eighteen months in prison does not appear to have deterred the Bryant family from a life of crime, as in 1812 Samuel, now aged twenty years, together with *SAMUEL BRITTON* aged just seventeen, were sentenced to two years imprisonment and fined one shilling each (equivalent to around one day's pay) for stealing wheat at Mangotsfield. Although no indication of the quantity of wheat was mentioned, it almost certainly represented little more than a few handfuls, and no doubt, the theft was more likely to have been brought about as a result of hunger rather than an attempt to obtain a financial reward. Not long afterwards, forty-year old *JOSEPH BRYANT* was sentenced to two years incarceration having been found guilty of attempted house breaking, and then it was the turn of twenty-three year old *DENNIS BRYANT* to enjoy the dubious benefits of prison life when he was charged with, and found guilty of setting fire to a hayrick. Finally before 1812 had a chance to give way to 1813, *ROBERT CRIBB* aged twenty years, was found guilty alongside his older brother *THOMAS*, of breaking into a "butcher's killing shop" and stealing a number of carcases. Before sentenced was passed, Robert was additionally charged with the more serious crime of horse stealing, and having been found guilty was condemned to be transported for fourteen years.

Throughout 1813, there was a steady parade of local criminals to and from the local County gaol, and the various assize courts, including *JAMES HATHWAY* arrested in Warmley near his home in the vicinity of Cock Road, and charged with a number of highway robberies, the bulk of which it was claimed had been perpetrated around the City of Bath.

Although the Kingswood Association, and in particular Thomas Bevan of the Bitton Cavalry, claimed to be the instigators of the increase in captured villains, most of the hard work fell upon the shoulders of the Bitton constables, Moses Batt and Charles Bull, who not only had to deal with the criminals themselves, they were frequently exposed to threats, and personal attacks by those who did not agree with their efforts to return law and order to the community they represented. During 1813, they received a complaint from *MARY TOWNSEND* that she had found bread stolen from her house in Oldland, and she suspected that the culprit was a certain *WILLIAM LACEY* whom she had previously seen loitering around near her home. Armed with this information, the two constables went out to search for Lacey, whom they soon found and apprehended on a charge of felony. Before the constables and the arrested man could return to the comparative safety of the Bitton lock-up, a group of Lacey's friends had gathered, and started an affray in an attempt to free the prisoner. Although they succeeded in their quest, their endeavours were rather futile as all, or the majority of the group, were known to the constables and within a matter of days *WILLIAM POWE, HENRY WILLIS, AMBROSE WILLIS, SAMUEL BRAIN, JOHN FRY, HANNAH JONES, SARAH LACEY,* and *HESTER BRITTON* were charged with the affray and with the attempted wounding of Charles Bull and Moses Batt. However as there seemed to be insufficient evidence to prosecute William Lacy and the male members of the rescue party, it was only the three women who "carried the can" and, being found guilty spent six weeks in prison.

The following year, Dennis Bryant the arsonist, turned to theft and burglary and somehow succeeded in stealing a bed from the home of a *STEPHEN BRITTON*. Whether it was required for his own use, or to be sold for a small monetary gain will now never be known, but as so often in this story we only discover what took place after the perpetrator had been caught and prosecuted, and that is exactly what happened to Dennis, as the records show that he was found guilty of that crime and sentenced to be transported to New South Wales for fourteen years. Although such a sentence sounds bad enough for the offence committed, it should not be forgotten that whatever was the number of years ascribed to the punishment, in reality the sentence was as good as life, as the chance of any transportee being able to save, after obtaining his freedom, sufficient funds to pay for a passage home were negligible. If the transportee had knowledge of seamanship, then he might stand a chance of working his passage, but even then what sort of homecoming would they receive, especially when few would recognize him after twenty years or so. Obviously some did make it home but they were certainly few and far between.

With a number of the more pious residents of Kingswood keen to try religion as a tool to help clear the district of the blackguards and miscreants, a Bible Association meeting was held on the 31st January 1814, in conjunction with the even more sanctimonious British and Foreign Bible Society. Although little if anything came of this meeting it attracted the attention of a *Gloucester Journal* reporter, who wrote:

"Such an institution was peculiarly wanted in a district which notwithstanding the various efforts made to improve it, still remains so uncivilized"

However uncivilized many of the inhabitants might have seemed to those who did not have to scrape together a living out of an extremely harsh environment, where poverty was the norm, and where escape from such drudgery, the constant hunger, and the lack of any kind of real sanitation was virtually impossible, for those who found themselves at the bottom of the pile, the unjust punishment handed out by the upper class also appeared to be uncivilized. For example, during the 1814 Lent Assizes held at Gloucester, twenty-five year old *ANN POWELL* was brought before the circuit Judge on the charge of stealing property from the home of a *MR. E. FRANKCOMB,* of Bitton, whilst her husband *JOSEPH* was charged with having received the goods, worth around £25 or the equivalent of about six months wages, knowing them to have been stolen. At the trial, Ann was found guilty and condemned to death, although this was subsequently commuted to two years imprisonment, whilst her husband was sentenced to seven years transportation. Undoubtedly, Ann should not have taken that which was not hers, but no defence was offered at the trial, and thus we will never know how desperate was her position, she may have had many mouths to feed, and no money to purchase the basis of a staple diet, she may have got into debt and was under pressure from the money lenders to repay the outstanding money, she may have of course simply carried out the theft on a whim, or because it gave her a needed adrenalin rush. None of this we will ever know but whether the punishment fitted the crime is another matter, and possibly a cause for the so-called uncivilized nature of the lower class inhabitants of Kingswood. On the 10th October 1814, the same journal published the following article:

"COCK ROAD GANG OF MARUDERS"

Information has recently been given to the local Magistrates that a gang of desperadoes infests the above named neighbourhood, to such an extent that no inhabitant felt safe in his bed, and that no traveller could pass along the Kingswood Road, without running the risk of being attacked and robbed. Accordingly, on last Sunday evening, a strong party of police officers from Bristol were despatched to Kingswood, in order to take these so called desperadoes into custody. The gang had, however, been previously warned of the approach of the Bristol police, and lay in wait, before attacking those brave policemen, and a desperate conflict ensued. The police officers retreated with their wounded, and appeared to have given back the ground to the gang, but in the early hours of the following day, the officers returned with a greater force, which was on this occasion well armed. Once again the villainous inhabitants of Kingswood lay in wait, but on this occasion the might of the police force prevailed, and seven men and two women were taken into custody and committed to Lawford's Gate Bridewell. Later that day and over the following days, other members of the gang were apprehended, including thirty year old Thomas Caines, his older brother George, arrested in Torbay. Both were committed to await trial at the next assizes to be held in Gloucester. Elizabeth Caines [alias Bush], the sister of George and Thomas, was sent to Shepton Mallet to appear before the magistrates at Ilchester on the charge of stealing six pigs from a butcher in Bath. The pigs had previously been found six months ago locked up in her parlour, and at the time a warrant had been issued but could not be executed with safety, owing to the strength of the gang"

Three months later in January 1815 the police, who were still looking for other so called members of the gang that "had committed such depredations in the neighbourhood of Bristol last summer, and who belonged to that sink of iniquity known as Cockroad," were rewarded with the news that *MOSES OWEN* and *JAMES CRIBB* were apprehended at Liverpool, through the spirited exertions of a *MR. PALMER* of Keynsham. Although little is known of this Mr Palmer, it is understood that he had suffered the loss of a number of horses, whom he believed had been stolen by these men and others, and who had put a value in excess of £700 (around £2,500,000 by today's values). Determined that they should not get away with their audacity, it would seem that Mr. Palmer somehow managed to track down the above named men, and have them arrested. Both men were subsequently brought before the Judges sitting at the assize courts, where Moses Owen was found guilty of horse stealing, and sentenced to death, being executed at Lancaster on the 22nd April 1815, whilst James Cribb escaped with his life, and was sent to the other side of the world on a one way ticket with no opportunity of returning home.

Most if not all of the above took place before Thomas Caines' arrest and imprisonment, which took place during the second half of 1815 and throughout the whole of the following year, and as we shall read, the coast was clear for brother Benjamin to get into trouble, in fact at around the time that Thomas was being freed in 1817, Benjamin was being incarcerated. This is however Thomas's story, who unfortunately appears not to have sharpened his wit's or ability, and had generally learned little or nothing from the two years in prison as, as soon has he had been released he was back to his old habits of trying to relieve the general public of their property without having first obtained their permission to do so, but his success rate had not improved. It would also seem likely that Thomas's memory had not improved as he either totally overlooked the fact that the Bitton Troop under the Captaincy of Thomas Bevan had been formed, and was still a very active deterrent in the area, or assumed that they restricted their activities to the Bitton area, or perhaps more likely considered himself to be able to outwit "Capt. Bevan." Whatever was going through his mind can only be supposition, but he certainly did not expect to be caught red-handed by a "private" of the Bitton Calvary (Troop) as he purloined four or five sacks of wheat grain from an inn at Cold Ashton. In a one to one struggle, the gallant private, succeeded in confiscating the grain and returning it to a *MR. DOLLING,* the rightful owner, whilst at the same time apprehending Thomas, and taking him to the lock-up in Bitton, some four miles away from the site of the arrest.

With Thomas only out of prison for a matter of weeks, the fact that he had been caught again after such little time must have dented his confidence, particularly as the man who had made the arrest was just a "private" in the hated Bitton Troop, and he was after all, a self styled Captain. Whatever Thomas's feelings were, there was nothing he could do about his incarceration, or the punishment likely to be doled out to him, which would not be long in coming as Thomas was scheduled to appear before the Magistrates in Gloucester at the 1817 Mid-summer Assizes. By chance his brother Benjamin was also making an appearance at the same session and it is almost certainly that this was going to be the last time the brothers would see each other. Thomas was the first to be called, and with his record well known to the court, there was little chance that he would be found anything other than guilty, or that the Judge would be lenient. After a very short hearing, and with authorities need to rid the community of yet another Caines, Thomas stood in the dock with a verdict of guilty, and the punishment of seven years transportation. Thus on the 20th December 1817, thirty-one year old Thomas followed his eldest brother to New South Wales aboard the good ship *Neptune*.

* * * * *

Although it is not at present certain, it is believed that Ann's next child was a boy, *ROBERT* born around 1788, as on the 1st December 1793, Benjamin Snr. and Ann had a further three children baptised at St. Mary's Bitton namely, Robert, Lydia and Benjamin. The latter would have only been a matter of a few months old; his sister would have been three, whilst Robert was possibly five years old. There seems to be no factual reason why the parents should again have a group christening, but as we have no information on Robert other than the date of his baptism, we might speculate that he had a serious life threatening childhood illness, and was accordingly baptised before his death, or perhaps Mr. & Mrs. Caines simply liked having group ceremonies, whatever was the reason will have to remain a mystery and we shall never know.

* * * * *

Sometime during 1790, a second daughter was born to Benjamin and Ann, and like her siblings before her, little if anything is known of *LYDIA,* particularly her childhood years, with the exception of her baptism when she was three years old, as mentioned above. What can be assumed is that as she grew up, she was surrounded by the harsh life of the world she had entered, although with petty crime almost a constant feature within the family, it is perhaps likely that she was much better off than her contemporaries. By her early teens, she had probably already seen two older brothers die of childhood illness, whilst a third brother had perished at the end of the executioner's rope. Family life, in the form of siblings was not going to get any better over the years to come, but by the time that Lydia had reached the age of seventeen, her independence and strong will took her out of the family fold, and into the arms of other criminals, to the extent a little while before her eighteenth birthday, she found that she was pregnant, giving birth to a son, *GEORGE CAINES (alias AVERY).* For reasons best known to herself, Lydia adopted her sister's strong anti views on marriage as a legal entity, and equally decided that such a status was simply not for her. Possibly, both sisters disliked the thought of being "owned" by a husband or, perhaps, seeing the way in which their father and their brothers rebelled against authority, they felt that this was a particular stance that could be taken by a woman. Whatever the reasons were neither of them seemed to relish, certainly during their formative years, the legal niceties or dubious security of being a bride, although as we have already discovered, sister Betty changed her opinion later in life. Whilst it may be reasonable to presume that Betty set up home with her common law husbands, we cannot be certain that Lydia ever actually lived with the father of her first born, nor can we be certain of his identity, other than he was presumably a Mr. Avery. As for Lydia herself she is something of an enigma, with very little known of her, although it is believed that ultimately she possibly went one better than her sister in losing partners to a life of slavery down-under, by seeing all three partners arrested and transported for various periods of time. With information somewhat sketchy, we can only presume that Avery was transported to Australia sometime around 1810, as during the early part of that decade, Lydia and her son moved in with *JASPER WILMOTT,* who was eight years her junior, and between them, they produced two children, *JAMES CAINES WILMOTT,* and *ELIZABETH CAINES WILMOTT,* although both of them dropped the Wilmott surname, and more often than not are known by the Caines surname, such was the influence of that family, and of its daughters. Almost certainly, Jasper was part of the Wilmot(t) family who were so actively involved in the high level of crime, which permeated the district for so many years, although exactly what part was played by him is unclear. What is known is that he was subsequently arrested around November 1817, sent for trial, and at the Michaelmas Assizes in Ilchester, he was found guilty, and sentenced to be transported for life, leaving these shores on the 28th March 1818, aboard the *"General Stuart"*. In due course on the 12th May 1831, Jasper Wilmott obtained his "Ticket of Leave", being described on the paperwork as being 5feet, 4inch tall, of fair/pale complexion, light brown hair, and hazel coloured eyes. He must have been a model prisoner, and well behaved including during the period immediately after receiving his ticket of leave, as three years later on the 20th February 1834 he received a Conditional Pardon. For the next nineteen years or so Jasper led a quiet lawful hardworking life before at the age of 55 years, he passed away on the 6th July 1853 at Sutton Forrest, in Australia, having never again seen his homeland or those he left behind. During those years he must have become reasonably prosperous as in his Will he left goods with a Probate value of just under £500, quite a fortune in those days.

With Jasper having been given a life sentence, Lydia knew that with three children to bring up she needed a new man in her life. Whilst she was fully aware of the life of crime that surrounded her very existence, and no doubt she took full use of its existence, and benefited from the illegal profits so secured, she was and remained a strong and independent woman, and would not like the idea of receiving financial help from her father and/or brothers, assuming of course that such help was on offer. However her eldest son was not far short of his tenth birthday, and had by now received a fairly good apprenticeship in the art of petty theft, pick-pocketing and the like, as well as an apprenticeship in the art of hat dying. No doubt with her own ability, plus a little help from her son, and probably from a new, and as yet unnamed live in partner she kept her family together. Exactly how long this third "husband" stayed around is not clear, but it is probable that they were together for about four or five years, before he too departed to the other side of the world. Sometime around 1824/25, Lydia met up with *ROBERT ENGLAND,* whom we will hear more of as the story unfolds, and it is probable that within a relatively short space of time they began living together. By now, Lydia was in her thirty-sixth year, and was about to undergo a metamorphosis inasmuch as her strong views on the undesirability of marriage were to go out of the window and some years before her sister she agreed to be married to Robert, and they made their solemn vows together on the 15th June 1826, at St. Mary the Virgin, Bitton. The following year, Robert Jnr. was born to a daughter of the Caines who had for many years been very adamant that like her sister, she was not going to get married.

Although, Lydia had, by this marriage, gained a certain amount of respectability, Robert was no angel, and quite often he was involved in acts of minor crime, or would benefit from others who may have taken the greater share of the risk. He obviously knew all about Lydia's background, and the background of her family, and the fact that his wife was not about to change the habits of a lifetime. As for Lydia herself, it is fairly obvious that she did nothing to dissuade her eldest son from participating in the family business, as by all accounts, George took to theft in quite a big way, but more of this later in the story.

* * * * *

The seventh child born to Benjamin and Ann was a boy, who arrived during 1793. Benjamin had always wanted a son to be named after him and to carry through his father's name. Tragically, having given their fourth child the name Benjamin, the little boy had died, and thus here was a golden opportunity to try again, and have a son named *BENJAMIN*. Anxious not to lose this child to the "Grim reaper", it is probable that both parents became somewhat overprotective of their latest offspring, and he almost certainly grew up as a rather spoilt child. No doubt like his brothers before him he was given the standard education in theft, extortion and other forms of crime. Not long after his eleventh birthday, Benjamin attended the funeral of his brother Thomas, who had not long died at the hands of the executioner. However, rather than remain in the background to cope with his own immature grief, whilst at the same time grappling with the important events of the day, he rather bizarrely decided, when the mourners were gathered around the coffin and the grave, to climb the churchyard wall, and whistle tunelessly throughout the whole proceedings. Questionably, was this the action of a young boy unable to show his grief in a more conventional way, in which case why did not one of his siblings comfort him and stop the embarrassing noise, or was it the actions of a spoilt child who considered his own importance to be much greater than the burial itself.

For the next few years Benjamin watched, with the enthusiastic eyes of a boy wanting to be a man, the antics of his eldest brother as he disappeared for days at a time and would then return with many stories to regale of adventures, near-misses, wine women and song, all of which simply encouraged Benjamin to find and participate in those marvellous adventures himself. All around him brothers, cousins and friends seemed to be having a great time, even though every now and then one or other of them would disappear for a while as they served their time in prison. Thus when his twenty-year-old brother Thomas is collecting friends and acquaintances together for a frontal rescue attack on the lock-up in Bitton, thirteen-year-old Benjamin ensured that he tagged along just for the fun of it. However, as manhood gradually overtook Benjamin, he was no longer regarded as a brat and as a nuisance by his brothers and cousins, and began to go on expeditions with them, and become more and more useful to them, especially in the form of extra muscle power.

By the time that his mentor and elder brother George, departed from his life, Benjamin had matured into a tall, for those times, twenty-two year old handsome young man, full of the ill-advised confidence of youth, who was determined to go one better than George and Francis, and make a good living out of crime against the elderly and the rich, and importantly not get caught. Accordingly over the next eighteen months or so, Benjamin applied his trade, with little success and/or reward, and despite his attempts to better himself, he had to realise by the time that 1816 turned into 1817, that he had to further change his *modus operandi* and to become much more hard nosed in his attitude.

Throughout the wet cold winter months, Benjamin spent time looking around the area in an attempt to find the most suitable house to burgle with the best and richest victim, and having picked out the property, he then went about choosing two roughnecks to help him put his plan into action, and on the 1st February 1817 he and his compatriots set off in the latter part of the evening, armed with a sword and a pistol, with the sole aim of breaking into the house of the elderly Miss *SARAH PRIGG,* of Bitton.

Unfortunately for young Benjamin, he was unable to put into practice his crime winning ideas, and he ended up faring no better, and probably much worse than his brothers, by not only bungling the burglary, but he also made a fatal and inexcusable mistake.

At his subsequent trial, Sarah Prigg said that although she usually lived by herself, she had had, at the beginning of 1817, for a week or two her nephew *JAMES EVANS* staying with her. On the evening of the 1st February she had retired to bed leaving James downstairs. Having fallen asleep, but she was not sure for how long, she was rudely awakened and in the candle light, saw the shape of three men, all of whom appeared to be wearing masks. Crying "MURDER" she jumped out of bed but was immediately knocked to the floor by one of the intruders who demanded her money. She declared that she had none, but not believing her and shouting "dreadful imprecations" they grabbed the clothes, which were lying at the foot of the bed, and began to rifle through the various pockets, emptied the contents and, throwing the apparel down on top of the elderly lady, they left the bedroom.

When James Evans gave his evidence, he said that he went to bed not long after his aunt had retired, but kept two or three candles burning as he wished to read before going to sleep. Disturbed by a noise, and the cry of "Murder" from his aunt, he got out of bed, put on his dressing gown and went to the landing where, near the top of the stairs he was confronted by three men who had just left his aunt's room, with one brandishing a sword, whilst another held a pistol. He distinctly heard a threat to kill him if he "wagged", which he presumed to mean that they would come back and kill him if he reported or described them to the police. Before he could take any action, he was seized by two of the men, bungled into his bedroom, and thrown on to the bed, before being fully covered by the quilt. Inexplicably, one of the intruders went over to the window, removed his mask and looked out. As he turned, James had managed to lift a corner of the quilt, and clearly saw the face of Benjamin Caines, whom he knew by sight as well as by reputation. All three men left his bedroom, and as far as he could detect, they went downstairs and left his aunt's dwelling house, but not before they had searched the cupboards and the rooms, and taken anything they believed could be exchanged for money. Waiting a while for the men to rifle the downstairs and leave the house and garden, James went to his aunt's bedroom and found her on the floor, extremely frightened and angry that she had been so accosted. Making his elderly aunt as comfortable as possible, James left the house to report the incident to the local constables, who immediately began to search the area. The following day Sarah Prigg, discovered the full extent of her loss, which included wearing apparel, silver tea-spoons, cash notes, Irish cloth shifts and sheets, and sundry other articles to the value of upwards of £30, (probably around £15,000 in today's valuation)

The first to be found and arrested was *HENRY WILMOT*, who at his trial claimed that he had kept watch whilst the burglary was being carried out, and had nothing whatsoever to do with the knocking over of Sarah Prigg, or the theft of the articles. It had been arranged that having acted as the lookout, he was to disappear and not to meet up with the others until the early hours of the following morning when he would receive his share. However, before he was able to carry out the plan he was apprehended.

The third member of the party, and the second to be apprehended was *JAMES BRYANT,* a man, it was recorded, "of the most forbidding aspect", which presumably related to not so much to his general demeanour, but to either a badly scarred or deformed face. It is also very likely that he was a man of little intelligence, as in a rather impudent child like way he tried to lie his way out of trouble by concocting a most implausible story at his trial, which was delivered without emotion or expression. According to James, he and Wilmot attended a club supper on the night of the 1st February 1817, and that they stayed together until 10.30pm when Henry Wilmot went home. There is then a gap of around an hour and a half, during which time; Bryant met up with a man called *MONK,* as together they walked to Wilmot's home, arriving there about midnight. Presumably Wilmot had either not gone to bed, or he was sufficiently aroused from his sleep to go down and let both Bryant and Monk into his house. For the next two or three hours, all three men sat talking, as around three o'clock, they left Wilmot's house and went to a field they knew where turnips were growing as they had decided to steal some turnips because they were hungry.

The Bitton constables had a very successful night, as not only did they catch Wilmot and Bryant, they also succeeded in arresting Benjamin. An entry in the Felons Register for the 13th August 1815, when Benjamin had previously appeared before the same magistrates bench, described him as being just over 5ft.7ins tall (against an average male height of just over 5ft.3in), with light brown hair, a fresh complexion, dark grey eyes, a short nose, turned up a little at the end, and long features. He had scars on two fingers of his left hand, and a scar on his left shin. His occupation was stated to be that of fish carrier, and it was noted that he could read a little. Whilst held in prison, it was reported that he had behaved very well, in other words he appears to have been a model prisoner, and there is no evidence to the contrary that he behaved any differently whilst he was incarcerated at the Bitton lock-up, and other similar institutions, prior to his arrival at the Gloucester Gaol on the 4th August 1817. For all his obvious bravado, Benjamin probably never had it in him to be a "real hard case" and whilst the spoiling of him by his parents, had probably led him to have an over inflated ego, it may say a great deal about his character, inasmuch as at no time does he appear to have used either his sword or pistol on the unfortunate Sarah Prigg, or her nephew, not even when he knew that he had been recognized, and thus his chances of getting away were extremely small. It is of course possible that his naiveté or sheer surprise or fear of being recognized, caused an understandable delay in his reaction, and as a consequence, he had no opportunity to draw his weapons. However, this explanation would seem unlikely as in his evidence, James Evans, stated that he saw the men brandishing a sword and a pistol, so both must have been drawn.

Whilst Benjamin had of course been up before the magistrates on previous occasions, as far as can be determined, the charges had related to fairly small and petty criminal acts, and in at least two instances, the charges had either been dropped, or dismissed altogether. Certainly at no time had Benjamin ever been accused of any form of physical violence to his victims and, as in this case, apart from Sarah being shoved to the ground by one or other of the three men, but not necessarily by Benjamin, no one had been seriously hurt, despite the fact that he was armed. In such circumstances, clemency may well have been a reasonable judgement to take into consideration, but of course we cannot overlook the fact that the Court was dealing with a Caines, and that basic fact would determine Benjamin's future.

Benjamin was without doubt guilty of the charge as sworn on the oath of Sarah Prigg, of having broken into her dwelling house in Bitton, and stolen various items of her property to the value of upwards of £30, and thus it came as no surprise that he was found guilty in a Court of Law. What did come as a surprise was the severity of the sentence handed out by the Judge who, in passing the death penalty stated that "in taking this decision he had very seriously considered ordering that the execution should take place immediately, and that his body should then be hung in chains in a public place, and there left to rot as an example to the rest of his infamous gang." Fortunately for Benjamin the Judge was actually having one of his better days, and decided, in the end, that in reality he wished to err on the side of leniency. Accordingly he ruled out the chains and commuted the sentence that Benjamin should just be hanged.

Whether Benjamin ever saw his brother Thomas, in the same prison, as the latter awaited a ship to take him to the penal colony in Australia, has not been recorded, but in the early morning of the 6th September 1817, Benjamin received the Last Rites in the Chapel of Gloucester Prison, before walking with much resignation, and a great deal of fortitude, to the scaffold over the Gate House. With the sentence having been carried out, and death certified by the prison doctor, Benjamin's body was handed over to his seventeen year old brother Samuel who, throughout that day and the following night, proceeded to carry, presumably by cart, his brother's body the forty miles or so back to their father's house in Oldland.

Although it was quite often the custom to lay the body out in the best room of the house, and for friends and neighbours to pay their respect, Benjamin Snr. decided to go one better, and with a touch of the theatricals, which veered somewhat into being a farce, the body of his son was laid out and exhibited in the parlour, with a small charge being made for those who had the rather macabre desire to look upon the earthly remains of young Benjamin. It was stated by his family that, the money so collected would be used by them to help defray the funeral expenses. Whether the local populace saw young Benjamin as some evil curiosity, or as some nineteenth century Robin Hood, or perhaps they had a personal desire to ensure that he was actually dead, will now never be known. However, what is known, is that the villagers, and others from far and wide, eagerly turned out in their multitudes to hand over their few and precious coppers, just to view the body. Within a matter of days, the Caines were amazed at how much money had been collected, and decided that they would arrange a funeral the like of which had never been seen before in the neighbourhood, or probably since.

On the day of the funeral, the remaining family gathered at the house of Benjamin Caines Snr., as did six women from the village, dressed entirely in white. At the appointed hour the six women carried the coffin from the house and as pallbearers, they and the cortege left for the two mile or so walk to St Mary's Bitton, with the coffin borne aloft. Throughout the journey, many onlookers, some of whom were, of course, Benjamin's criminal friends and their relatives, turned out to pay their respects, flanked the procession, and as it passed, joined the rear of the cortege. Other people stood out of pure curiosity, and the human desire to be nosey, whilst others genuinely mourned the passing of this young man, convinced that he had been dealt with extremely harshly. A few in the crowd hissed and booed, but were quickly turned upon by others, who ensured that those who showed their displeasure were given the same treatment. By the time that the possession reached St Mary the Virgin, there were sufficient people already there and in the cortege to more than fill the church. During the service, the congregation listened to the vicar who had few words to say about the virtues of young Benjamin, but instead preached a solemn sermon using as his theme *"let him who stole, steal no more"*.

Outside, many friends had quietly walked out of the sermon, and joined the abundant onlookers, and friends who had gathered in the churchyard where, it might be added there was less of a sombre mood, but more of a carnival atmosphere, which was being encouraged by copious amounts of ale and beer. Gradually all of the official and unofficial mourners came out of their sombre habits, and began to mingle with those out in the churchyard who had long since begun to drink to the health of Benjamin and, with plenty of money in the kitty, all who wished to partake in the merry-making were soon able to enjoy the liberal flow of alcohol, which circulated around the graveyard throughout the remainder of the day. Such was the general mood of enjoyment experienced by those who were there, that the reason why they were there became lost in a haze of intoxication, and before anyone realised, or even cared, day had turned to night, and still Benjamin's coffin rested all alone in the church. Eventually as the supply of alcoholic beverages began to run dry, the fact that they were there for the purpose of laying to rest the mortal remains of their son, brother, friend began to dawn upon them, and there was a frenzied rush to obtain as many candles as possible. In due course, the coffin was carried from the church aisle and out to the northern side of the churchyard, where the grave of Thomas Caines had already been opened. With candles held aloft, giving what little light they could, and with no one there to give a eulogy, Benjamin's body was committed to the ground, in the grave already occupied by his brother for the past thirteen years, whilst his parents, and siblings looked on with grief in their hearts.

At just twenty-four years of age, Benjamin had paid the ultimate price for his criminal actions, but more particularly because he had been born a Caines. Henry Wilmot and James Bryant, his co-conspirators went free.

Such was the anger over the complete injustice of the sentence that over the next few months, those who remained loyal to the Caines, embarked upon a vicious rampage against persons considered to be part of the "establishment". Unfortunately some of the victims chosen had no voice in the matter, as the loyalists seemed to take a great delight in venting their misplaced anger upon the animals who belonged to people considered as the establishment. In one such instance, the horse belonging to *GEORGE HASKINS* the Bitton Constable, was crippled after having had the large tendon at the back of both of it's hind legs severed by a knife. *HENRY WILLIS*, one of the lesser members of the group, was subsequently identified as the person who carried out this inhumane attack on the constable's horse. Possibly in his own warped mind, he may have chosen the horse as an easy target, or he may have assumed that his actions would enhance his reputation. Certainly Henry did not suddenly become the most popular fellow in the area, and to a certain extent he found himself somewhat ostracised by his acquaintances. Whether he was responsible for the next attack has not been recorded, but without doubt the second assault carried his hallmark, as some weeks after the attack on the constable's horse, his cow was similarly treated, and mangled. In general, during this period of vindictiveness, corn ricks were put to the torch; houses, gardens and fields in the area were plundered for anything that could be easily carried away, and despicably other animals were either killed or maimed. Having eventually exhausted their fury, the heinous crimes finally began to peter out, and the establishment and their animals could start to relax. However, despite the nature and direction of these wicked acts, and despite there being at least one person under suspicion, not one of the perpetrators was ever brought to account.

Whilst it is relatively easy to connect the above crimes with the injustice meted out to Benjamin, we must not overlook the fact that at the time he paid the ultimate price for his crime, there were probably around twenty to twenty-three residents of Bitton domiciled in the Gloucester Gaol, and thus the plundering of fields and gardens, plus the killing of animals may have been brought about by necessity, to feed those left behind whilst perhaps the main, or one of the main bread-winners was incarcerated some forty miles or so away. This is not to excuse the terrible acts of vandalism perpetrated on defenceless animals, but it might be part of the much wider basis that was the root cause of the lawlessness that was so rife at the time. Some of those involved were *GEORGE BRITTON* and *WILLIAM BAKER* both accused of highway robbery, both found guilty of the charge, and both sentenced to death, but reprieved at the last moment, having the sentenced reduced to transportation for life. George Britton, spent ten months on board a rotting hulk, before he left for Botany Bay, William probably languished in a different hulk for much longer as his passage details have not yet been traced, he may of course even died whilst awaiting transportation.

SAMUEL BRAIN (alias BLACK) and *FRANCIS BRITTON* were charged with the theft of poultry, but although both were found guilty only Samuel went to prison, and served out his twelve months sentence, Francis somehow obtained a proclamation so that all of the charges against him were subsequently dropped. After spending a period of time in prison, *THOMAS ALBERRY (alias MAGGS)* was acquitted of stealing his stepfather's life savings. Around about the same time that he was in prison, so were *GEORGE WILMOT, GILES WILMOT, THOMAS SWEET, EDWARD PEACOCK, RICHARD MORETON,* and *HENRY MORETON* all charged with housebreaking, and all ended up less luckier than Thomas Alberry.

JAMES BAKER, JOSEPH PARKER (alias EVANS), JOSEPH BRYANT, ISAAC BALLARD were each charged with breaking into *THOMAS PRATTEN'S* home, whilst *HENRY WILLIS*, (the same Henry who carried out the attacks on the constable's horse, and the same Henry who with Thomas Caines and another had tried and failed to rescue Isaac Cox) and his brother, *AMBROSE WILLIS* were charged with attempting to rescue Thomas Pratten from Constable Charles Bull. Perhaps Thomas was too friendly with the despicable Henry, and those who disagreed with the injuring of the animals were carrying out a little retribution of their own. Looking back at these instances it would seem that Henry Willis was either very dim witted, or a "hot-head" who never learned.

So the list went on with the brothers *JOHN and JOSEPH ETTLE* being accused of stealing two ducks, but with lack of evidence, presumably it had been eaten, both were acquitted of the charge. The unfortunate *BENJAMIN CRIBB* was discovered by the local constables with a quantity of hay, which although it was being used to help feed his somewhat emaciated beast, nevertheless did not belong to him. Accordingly he was arrested, charged, found guilty, and sent to prison. Even more unfortunate were *HENRY PHIPPS* (twenty-two years' old) and *SAMPSON COOKE,* who both appeared at the 1817 Lent Assizes. The former was found guilty of stealing a quantity of clothes, from a dwelling house owned by one of the locals who aspired to being part of the establishment, and given seven years transportation. After spending the best part of six hot summer months, in a stinking hulk, Henry was then bundled onto the sailing vessel *Batavia* As for the luckless twenty-three year old Sampson, his punishment was fourteen years transportation for having been found culpable of the theft of a hay knife, valued at just two shillings. [0.10p] He left onboard the *Ocean 11* on the 21 August 1817, with both villains bound for New South Wales.

* * * * *

Having now lost two sons to the work of the hangman, one to natural causes, and two sons sent to the other side of the world, Benjamin and Ann were, in 1817, left with just three sons and two daughters, plus the remnants of their entourage to look after them in their old age. With brother Robert, the white sheep of the family, and doing his own thing, the mantle of leadership responsibility now fell on the shoulders of *SAMUEL CAINES*, who in the main earned a living working underground as a coal miner. Born in 1795, and named after his father's eldest brother, Samuel was baptised at the age of twenty years at St Mary the Virgin, Bitton, on the 17th September 1815, together with his younger brother, *JOSEPH* and elder sister *SARAH*, who were twelve and seventeen years old respectively. Previously, by the time that Samuel reached ten years of age, he had been taught many of the tricks involved in the petty crimes that were so rife in the area at the time, and had no doubt watched and observed his elder brothers carrying out their relentless pursuit of money making schemes, although his attention to the many methods used was probably weakened by the recent death of his brother, and the frightening stories woven around Francis' life and death as recounted by the older members of his family. The fact that his brother had not only been caught, but found guilty and hanged, undoubtedly had a huge effect upon the impressionable Samuel, and it is reasonable to surmise that he spent many hours as a young boy working underground, learning the skills, and understanding the nature of the extremely hard work involved of being a miner. No doubt from time to time as he grew older and stronger he would have benefited from the family taught skills, by either working independently, or together with one of his brothers and/or cousins. By the time he reached his late teens, Samuel's main preoccupation was courting *HANNAH*, who lived up the hill in Kingswood. Believed to have married his sixteen-year-old sweetheart at Holy Trinity Church Kingswood around 1816, the couple ultimately had between them three daughters, *MARY* (born c1817), *ANN* (born c1820) and *ELIZA* (born c1822). It is believed that Hannah and her three daughters were christened all together at Holy Trinity sometime during 1831/32.

Having married, and acquired a family, Samuel probably found himself under increasing financial pressure to provide the minimum basic requirements of life, including putting enough food on the table. With his family background, Samuel was unable to resist the opportunities which came his way to steal either food, money or articles that could be easily converted into money, and this led, as it had with many who had gone before him, to his downfall. During the spring of 1832, Samuel was arrested and charged with theft, and sent for trial. Found guilty, the Magistrates sitting at the Gloucester City Summer Assizes, gave no consideration to the existence of his young wife and three small children at home, and receiving no lenience from the Bench, who no doubt considered Samuel's surname to be the absolute requisite for him to be an undesirable, ordered that he should be sentenced to transportation to the colonies for a minimum of seven years. With no right of appeal, Samuel boarded the sailing vessel *"Mary"* on the 4th September 1832, bound for New South Wales, which he reached in January 1833, whilst behind him he had left his thirty-two year old wife to bring up by herself, three young daughters, with little or no chance of ever seeing her husband again.

However much injustice Samuel felt about the severity of his conviction, he appears not to have allowed his frustration to work to the surface, he knuckled under the impositions of his transportation and the fact that physically there were going to be many years of hard toil ahead of him as he was allocated to work for the Australian Agricultural Company at Port Stephens, a settlement some 100 miles north of Sydney. During his sojourn at Port Stephens, he educated himself by either learning to read and write or by improving those skills; in addition he appears to have become something of a reformed character, as by 1842 Samuel is recorded as a freeman, working as a hospital dispenser. With more than ten years past since he last set eyes on his childhood sweetheart, and little or no chance of him ever being able to raise enough money to return to old England, assuming of course that he actually wanted to return, as there is no evidence that he ever wrote home, Samuel turned his attention to female company, and by the mid 1840's he was living with a Jane, (no other details known of her) and in 1847 there is a baptismal record of a Jane Cain(s) the daughter of Samuel Cain(s) and Jane.

As far as can be determined, Samuel's reformed character meant that he was able to get on with his new life with Jane and his fourth daughter, as an honest upright citizen of the new found colony of Australia, living for a further 36 years, before dying in 1883 at the old age of 86, in Liverpool New South Wales. If his given age is correct then it casts a doubt over the accuracy of his birth year, alternatively his quoted age may be inaccurate.

What of Hannah and their three daughters, who had been left back in Bitton to make the best of a bad job? Details of their lives are scant and outside of the scope of this book, but through the kindness of Mrs. Greta Pearce, a descendant of Samuel, the following letter is reproduced.

On the 22nd November 1876, the three sisters through an intermediary wrote to their cousin James Caines Willmot in New South Wales the following letter:

Dear Cousin, This day I have took this opertunity to write these few lines to you and all my relations hoping this my letter will find you Dear Cousin and all our relations in as Good Helth as it leaves us all at present thank God for it. Dear Cousin, I should be greatly oblige to you if you would be so kind as to make known these letter to your Uncle Mr Samuel Cairns which is my Father for me and my two sisters are verry desirous to know how him is and where him is it's a long time since we have heard about him its above twenty years for we cannot get the least knowledge of him from any of our relations nor any one else for no satisfaction. We seen a man who was a native of Bristol his name was George Little him told me and my Mother and my sister Eliza that he was verry mutch aquainted with my Father and him told us that above 20 years ago that someone had wrote a letter and sent him to my Father saying that my Mother his wife was dead at that time but it was all a falsehood but know my Mother is dead. She died on the 28 of November in the year of our Lord 1875. She have been dead a 12 month this month. Dear Cousin we sisters is three and we have been and now verry desiorous to hear about our Father if you can make him known unto us and we to him we should be greatly oblige to you, there is 18 gran children we do know that a Father is near to children and the children is near and sprecious to the Father. Dear Cousin you mind and find him out if him is a living and if he is dead let us know and let us know what part he is in and where he is, it is verry likeley that Father might remember his children Names their Names is as follows the eldest is Mary Caines or Cairns the Mother (of) 6 children, Ann the Mother of 9 and Eliza the Mother of three verry induterous and hardworking children, we heard he was in Cydney and again in Stephen Port town and there again at Burramacer Road.

Now Dear Cousin we do put all of our dependence in you to do the best as you can to complete this job for us us and if you cannot do it send and let us know as soon as you can for we have two Neighbours as been in Cydney about 4 months and we shall send to them and they will have him in the Human cry.

No more at present from your affectionate Cousins Mary & Ann and Eliza Caines or Cairns.

When the above letter was written, Samuel would have been around 81 years of age, and as we know, was living in Liverpool, rather than in Sydney or Port Stephen, as believed by his daughters. Therefore whether their letter, and/or its contents ever reached their Father is open to speculation, if it had, would his natural fatherly instinct have encouraged him to respond, or had the passage of 46 years dulled his emotions, unfortunately we shall never know, all that we are left with is a minute part of the human tragedy caused by the brutality inflicted upon the lower classes, by the establishment, in their quest to rid England of its criminals.

After Samuel, there was a relatively short period of around three years before the aging Benjamin Snr, and Ann became parents again, when their third daughter *SARAH* was born in 1798. It is known that Sarah certainly grew in to womanhood, as she was baptised aged seventeen years, at St Mary's Bitton on the 17th September 1815, alongside her two brothers *SAMUEL* and *JOSEPH,* but regrettably that is all that has so far been found out about her, and it is therefore possible that her life was cut short by illness, and that was why she was baptised at that time.

The last known child to have been born to Benjamin and Ann, was *JOSEPH* born during 1803, some twenty-six years after his eldest brother was born. Together with Samuel and Sarah, he was baptised at St. Mary's Bitton on the 17th September 1815, and regrettably that is all that we know of this, their tenth child.

# # # # #

THE PARTNERS AND CHILDREN OF ELIZABETH (BETTY) CAINES.

The first recorded man in Betty's life was Timothy Bush, who is believed to have been the son of *GILES* and *ELIZABETH BUSH*. If this is correct then Timothy was born around 1779, and had at least one sister, *Harriet* baptised at St. Mary's on the 20th May 1797. During 1805, Betty gave birth to a son whom they christened James on the 2nd December 1805, also at St. Mary's Bitton. Importantly, the parents or perhaps Betty, decided that James should also be given her surname, and thus as he grew up he was always known as James Caines Bush, or more frequently, as he became older, simply as James Caines (alias Bush), a name, which occurred more frequently after his father had been transported to the penal colonies in 1813. At the impressionable age of eight, James found understandable comfort in spending time with his cousins, having no doubt already received a sound grounding in the art of petty theft, and was almost certainly a difficult child to bring up, especially as it would seem that he was not necessarily the "brightest in the class". Not only did he and his brother Francis suffer from the loss of having their father forcibly removed forever from them, they also had to cope with the fact that in a relatively short space of time, their mother was introducing them to a new substitute father. Somehow James coped, as far as we can see, with these major changes in his young life but, at the age of ten, whilst the pain of losing his father was still relatively fresh in his mind, he found that Uncle George was also being taken away from him, as he was additionally sent away for life, to that strange world that existed somewhere else. Then, just two years later, and still only at the tender age of twelve, two more major calamities fell upon his immature shoulders, with one of his favourite uncles, Benjamin being hanged, whilst another favourite Uncle Thomas followed his father and older uncle to another world beyond his imagination. Perhaps, understandably James, as he entered his teenage years, was emotionally and mentally scarred and that scarring assuredly had a lasting effect upon the future behaviour of this young man. As he went through those painful adolescent years, James frequently found himself in minor skirmishes and scrapes, but nothing that bad that seems to have warranted a brush with the law, and certainly there is no record of James having been arrested or charged with any event, however all was about to tragically change.

* * * * *

The 27 November 1824 was a typical cold dank day, which did not improve with the fall of darkness, as a blanket of murky gloom descended over the small village of Warmley. Within the bar room of the *Tennis Court Inn*, a fire burned brightly as it tried to create enough heat to dry out the customers' damp outer clothes and to keep them warm, as either singularly, or as in groups, the patrons told their stories, whilst supping their ale, to whoever would listen, as the flame of the candles flickered in the smoke ladened atmosphere, with each draught of cold air that swept around the room every time the bar room door was opened. Drinking in the bar on his own at this time was the local village pound keeper, *ISAAC GARDEN* although his name may have been spelt as *GORDEN*. With many people owning grazing animals in the nineteenth century, and with there being unfenced common land, many of these animals were, from time to time, found wandering the streets of the village, or grazing other peoples land, and accordingly the parish appointed a secure area of land called a pound, and a pound keeper to collect the vagrant animal, place it in the pound, and to collect the appropriate fee when the rightful owner came to collect his property. Also in the bar on that fateful night was James, and a group of his young and not so young drinking companions, all of whom were probably blood related, namely *ROBERT ENGLAND, ISAAC BRITTON, MARK WHITING, THOMAS WILMOT, SAMUEL*

PEACOCK and a middle-aged man, *FRANCIS BRITTON,* the father of eighteen year old Isaac.

A day or so previously, an employee of *JOHN BRAIN,* a local farmer, had found a stray horse on land belonging to his master, and having reported the matter, was instructed by Mr. Brain to call in Isaac Garden, with a view to taking it away to the village pound situated just behind the *Tennis Court Inn,* which he did, and was soon able to identify the animal as belonging to the said Francis Britton. Once in the pound the only way in which the animal could be released was for Francis Britton to pay the appropriate "fine" for having allowed his horse to have wandered onto other peoples' property. Francis had presumably paid the relevant charge but in doing so it obviously wrangled him, and he probably felt that Isaac Garden could have been a little more sympathetic and perhaps even have turned a blind eye to the charge. Thus finding himself in a small room with his protagonist, however innocent Isaac Garden was in just carrying out his job, was a perfect opportunity for Francis to start his mumblings, and to talk about the pound keeper as though he was not there. With the courage of numbers, Francis' teenage son, Isaac, decided to put in his "pennyworth" to ensure that his namesake would rise to the bait who, although obviously outnumbered, was not prepared to have his good name taken in vain, and soon there was bad-humoured banter filling the air. By now the other members of the drinking group had added their comments to try and further inflame the argument, and to make Mr. Garden feel as uncomfortable as possible.

To add weight to the displeasure already being suffered by the poor pound keeper, small pieces of broken clay pipe and dirt from their shoes were now used by some of the drinking group as missiles aimed at Isaac Garden, although how many actually hit him was never recorded. Subsequently it was claimed that around this time, James Caines Bush allegedly swore at Garden and threatened that he would "knock Garden's brains out", and that Robert England had shouted that "it was a damned shame that Garden had impounded his friend's horse in the first place, and that as a result he should now be given a good hiding". Outnumbered, and fearful of his personal safety, even though the disturbance appears to have been no more or no worse than verbal abuse, accompanied perhaps, by some pushing and shoving, Garden decided that the best course of valour was to make a tactical withdrawal and, manoeuvring as carefully as possible through the bar room crowd, Isaac Garden left the inn, turned to his left, and entered a lane which crossed Gibbet Patch, heading towards Grimsbury Farm. Undoubtedly, the pound keeper drinking on his own without a single friend to give him moral support, must have found the whole experience extremely intimidating, which would seem to make his subsequent actions all the more surprising.

The next set of events are unfortunately clouded in mystery and aggravated by speculation, with the only known recorded facts being that in a few minutes ~ certainly no more than five ~ after he left the *Tennis Court Inn,* Isaac Garden returned to what he must have now presumed was the comparative safety of the bar room, and in addition he claimed to have been knocked to the ground by Thomas Wilmot, but does not claim to have been hurt by Wilmot's actions. Therefore something worse must have occurred outside the public house which prevented Garden from hastening home as quickly as his legs would carry him, and which caused him to decide that it was better to "run the gauntlet" of verbal abuse or even worse back in the bar room. Some have claimed that when he left the inn he was followed by Caines and Whiting, but as neither man had any particular gripe with Garden, other than having joined in with their cronies to verbally bully the poor pound keeper, and to enjoy the sport of intimidation, it would seem unlikely that these two men, on their own accord would chase after Garden and cause him to be sufficiently frightened not to continue on his way home. It is of course possible that they may have threatened his family with violence if he did not return to the inn, but for what purpose, almost certainly they knew where he lived and could have gone to his house at anytime they chose. In addition such a threat in the days when there was still a rather strange code of ethics amongst most criminals, to keep arguments, and their solutions between the men, would make such a theory highly unlikely. Alternatively they may have taunted him with uncomplimentary comments, which so offended his principles or code of honour, that Garden felt that he had no choice but to return; again it would seem most unlikely that something could have been said outside the inn that was so offensive or pertinent to Isaac's sensibility that he turned and went back into the "den of iniquity" the cauldron of hate. Whether either Caines or Whiting followed Garden along the pathway will now never be known, but as it would have appeared to serve no purpose, the probability is that they did not. What of Thomas Wilmot who, according to Garden, was the lad who pushed him over, or in Garden's words, "knocked me to the ground". Was he implying that he had been punched, or was it a shove, neither is made clear, and as the pound keeper recovered sufficiently to crawl/walk back to the inn, any injuries that he might have suffered appear to have been minimal, although it has to be accepted that a blow to the head, for example, may induce a delayed reaction, and the true extent of Garden's injuries may not have been immediately visible, or even noticed by Garden. Whilst it is true that the bar room was much nearer to Garden at the time of being knocked to the ground, than was his home, most people would, in such circumstances, head for home and safety, rather than return to the source of his humiliation, and the place where young men where determined to make his life as unbearable as possible.

With there being no evidence that any of the drinking group, other than Wilmot, had followed Isaac Garden outside, the reason why he returned to the *Tennis Court Inn* can only be guessed, did he want to say sorry; did he feel unwell, particularly after his fall? Either is a possibility, but as upon his return, he continued to drink then it is reasonable, in the case of the latter possibility, that he was well enough to have struggled home. He may of course continued drinking so as to build up sufficient "Dutch Courage" to risk any confrontations with the drinking group or even he may have considered isolating Francis Britton on his way home, and to settle the score on a one-to-one basis. All that can be said is that Garden left the inn, returned a few minutes later, claiming that he had been assaulted, continued drinking in the presence of Britton, Britton, Whiting, Peacock, England Wilmot and Caines, and probably other independent witnesses, without any further trouble, and waited for the seven drinking companions to leave to finish their evening's drinking session at Francis Britton's house, although by now Francis was probably so inebriated that he had no idea whether he did or did not verbally hand out the invitation to his young friends at sometime during their stay at the inn. Armed with jugs full with at least six quarts of beer, four or five of the drinking party staggered out of the public house and vacillated their way along the turnpike road, to Francis Britton's cottage. As for the others, which were probably James Caines, Mark Whiting, and possibly one other, they left the inn, and unencumbered by jugs of ale, made their independent way through the dark damp gloom of this November evening. It is known that the second group arrived at the cottage a short while after the first group, and it is believed that the smaller group had made their way via the footpath which crossed Gibbet Patch, but the nature of the inclement weather meant that there were very few independent witnesses around who actually were able to identify with certainty who went where. By now the victim of the earlier verbal abuse decided that the coast was clear, and accordingly Isaac Garden, left the warmth and comfort of the hostelry, went out of the public house, in to the gloom, turned left and entered the same pathway he had left an hour or so previously on his way home.

Around about twenty yards or so along the footpath was a stile that was nearby two adjoining cottages, the homes of the Ponting and the Lewis families, both partially built with the use of hard shiny blocks, being the waste product of the nearby spelter works. When subsequently asked by the local constabulary, both Mrs Ponting and Mrs Lewis stated that at sometime during the last hour of that day they had been disturbed by the noise of a group of people laughing and talking in a jocular manner. After a few moments the noise abated and there appeared to be complete silence, during which time they both claim to have heard a faint, but nevertheless audible sound that sounded like someone crying out "Murder". Almost as though in unison, the women are reported to have stated that after hearing the ill-defined cry, there was a moment of silence followed by the sound of blows, which initially made them think that a person was trying to resist an attack, but afterwards the sound gave the impression that the blows were being struck on a "dead thing". Again there was a moment of silence, broken on this occasion by a voice that exclaimed *"There thou be'est"* followed by a hollow laugh. Both women believed that the sound they heard came from the direction of the stile, which connected the pathway with Grimsbury Lane; neither of the women looked out of their cottages, or investigated the strange noises, or explained why their stories were so identical.

At the other end of the footpath the public house was closed for the night and, unlike either Mrs Ponting or Mrs Lewis, most sensible people had retired to their beds, as the dark foreboding outline of the *Tennis Court Inn* was covered by a cold, dank, still air of this November night, which wherever you looked, seemed to pervade every inch of the surrounding countryside, hiding some familiar objects and shapes, and contorting others in to weird configurations, that could send a chill down one's spine. Through this uninviting arena came a coal miner, huddled up as best he could against the cold and damp, on his way home from a long fourteen hours shift of hacking coal from a twenty-inch seam, whilst lying on his side. His body ached with the strain of his work, and the discomfort of his job, he was hungry, tired, wet and cold, and all that was on his mind was the comfort, however sparse that might have been, of his home. He passed the familiar gaunt dark shadow of the inn, made even more haunting by the invasive mist, which caused the whole building to drip with cold drops of water, and entered the wet muddy footpath which led him home across Gibbet Patch. As a coal miner, he was used to the sight of all forms of unpleasant gruesome deaths, but on this particular night of nights, even he was unprepared for the sight that greeted him as he was just about to wearily climb the stile, almost in sight of home. Realising at once that he had stumbled across a body that even though was face down appeared to be badly battered, was lying in a gore of blood, and was almost certainly dead; he called out for help, and for the local constable to be called.

By the time the constable arrived, a number of local people had responded to the miner's call, and had already identified the body as being that of Isaac Garden, and soon the story of the previous evening's altercation, involving Garden and a known group of seven men in the *Tennis Court Inn* began to spread amongst those who were there, and by daylight the expanded and no doubt exaggerated details had become common knowledge. A cursory examination of the body indicated that the victim had received a massive blow to the base of the skull, plus what appeared to be two knife wounds to the forehead. Near to the body, a clasp knife with a broken blade was found, as was a garden post, both of which showed signs of having been splashed with blood.

The weak, watery, winter sun provided little light as it struggled up over the horizon some seven hours or so after Isaac Garden's body had been removed from the scene of his unfortunate demise, and it was probably an hour after sunrise when the constable returned to the spot just below the stile where the terrible event had taken place. Searching for clues, or more particularly evidence that would convict the seven men involved with the murder, after all there could be no other explanation other than one or more of the drinking seven had struck the fatal blow, and with a Caines involved, there was already a guilty prime culprit. Despite the fact that many persons had passed that way during the previous twenty-four hours, the constable was, with the power of foresight, able to pick out in the mud, a particular set of footprints, which he considered belonged to the murderer, plus in addition there was in the mud, near to the position of the body, an imprint where someone had obviously sat down. In addition, within this imprint, there was a further smaller shape that the constable considered was the outline of a patch where the owner's trousers had once been mended.

Armed with this evidence, and the names of the seven drinking companions involved in the altercation with the unfortunate Mr Garden, the constable set about, the relatively simple task of taking them into custody. By the end of the day, six of the seven men were being housed in the new windowless lock-up, euphemistically known as the *"Blind House"*. Then without the aid of any form of forensic science, the men's clothing was examined, and very quickly the constabulary came to the conclusion that there was one of those there who was wearing patched breeches, and that from memory the shape and size of the patch matched the muddy impression adjacent to where the body had been discovered, and that person was none other than Mark Whiting. Furthermore, spots of blood were found on his coat, and on the coat belonging to James Caines Bush. In addition, the knife was identified as belonging to Robert England, and "independent" witnesses confirmed that England had been in possession of that knife on the day that Isaac Garden met his maker.

As far as the apparent blood spots on the coat belonging to James Caines Bush are concerned, he continually claimed that they had been caused by splashes of boiling pitch, which would seem to indicate that the spots were dark in colour, rather than the expected brighter red of fresh blood, but true to form, no one appeared to be prepared to listen to, let along accept the word of a Caines.

In order for the due process of law to proceed, all of the men needed to be charged on oath before *JOSEPH PARKER* of Upton Cheyney, the local Justice of the Peace, and accordingly on the second day following Isaac Garden's death, all six men were escorted by the local constabulary, from Warmley, through Oldland Common, Bitton, and then on up the hill to the village home of the JP. They were probably conveyed to the meeting in an open horse-drawn wagon, with the constables riding their individual horses alongside, all under the control of Sergeant *GEORGE HASKINS* of Kingswood. According to the sergeant, as the wagon proceeded along part of the journey, he saw Mark Whiting deliberately cause his face to be scratched by a hedgerow briar to a sufficient depth to bleed, and that having done so, he then dabbed the blood with his coat flap, this being the same flap on which Isaac Garden's blood stains had been earlier noticed. As quickly as possible, Sergeant Haskins ordered the party to halt, and dismounting from his horse he climbed up on to the open wagon, seized Whiting and, drawing his knife, he immediately cut away the blood stained part of the prisoner's coat, placing the item in his pocket, so that it could be preserved as evidence. He then ordered Whiting to sit down, and once he had re-mounted his steed, he then instructed the wagon driver, and the other constables to proceed to Upton Cheyney.

Sergeant George Haskins appears to have been, according to other available records, a resourceful policeman, but it is just possible that his resourcefulness enabled him, or even caused him to bend the rules, so that he would appear to his superiors to be just the man for the job. It is of course quite possible that the above story is correct, but if that is true then it creates a number of suppositions that cannot be ignored. With the vigorous growth of summer over, the briars/brambles in the hedgerows would, by the month of November, have lost their impetuous, and whilst still retaining their thorns, it would have been much more difficult to find one at the right height and strength to penetrate the facial bearded skin, to have caused much more than a superficial scratch, let alone one which would have been sufficiently deep enough to have drawn blood. Even though it has been claimed that Mark Whiting came from a better class of family, and by implication was better educated than his drinking companions, it is unlikely that in his then state of shock at having been treated like a criminal, for the past thirty hours or so, that he would have had the foresight to look out for a briar on his side of the cart, whilst it continued on its journey, for that briar to have been caught and forced against his hairy cheek sufficiently hard enough to scratch the skin and cause his blood to flow, is hard to comprehend. Furthermore, Whiting would have had to judge the self inflicted injury quite correctly so as to have produced sufficient quantity of blood to match or disguise the existing stains on the flap, a task that seem most improbable for this young man, particularly whilst he is travelling in an escorted cart, with five other prisoners. In any case, Whiting must have surely considered himself, at the time, to have been an innocent man, and thus why put his probity in danger by taking such a risk, particularly if, as has been claimed Mark was better educated than his companions. What of course may well have happened was that accidentally Whiting was scratched by the briar and, as an automatic reaction, he simply wiped his face with the nearest piece of fabric available to him, ie the flap of his coat, and that a rather over zealous Sergeant Haskins, by chance noticed what had happened, or more likely the act of wiping the blood, and chose to put a totally different interpretation on to what he had seen, because that suited the case, rather than give the benefit of the doubt to someone who Haskins already believed was guilty as charged.

It will be recalled that both Mrs Ponting, and Mrs. Lewis made identical statements regarding what they had heard from the lane outside of their cottages, including their apparent ability to distinguish between the sound of blows being fought off, and the sound of blows on a "Dead Thing", and their ability to identify the word "Murder" when said as a faint cry. There is of course nothing in the records to indicate or to establish that they did indeed have such abilities, but neither is there anything in the records to say that they did not, and thus we are left once again with speculation as to what might or might not have happened. Nor do the records indicate when their statements were taken, but as the miner found the body and then immediately called out for the police to be fetched, it is reasonable to presume that their statements were made quite some while after the body had been identified, and the story of the previous night's altercation had been made public knowledge. If, as suggested by these two ladies, Isaac Garden succeeded in warding off some of the earlier blows, then almost certainly, bruising would have occurred on his arms and hands, but nowhere is any reference made to any bruising, and whilst accepting of course the lack of forensic evidence, even in the early part of the nineteenth century there were many surgeons and pathologists around who were available to be called in to examine the body where there had been a sudden violent death, and if they had then surely any such bruising would have been noted and recorded. Perhaps the two ladies were uncertain of what they heard, assuming that they actually heard something, and decided to be a little fanciful in their stories for reasons best known to themselves. Almost two hundred years later, it is impossible to know what those ladies heard or did not hear, but being as charitable as possible and assuming that they made their statements with a civic duty in mind, it does seem that their joint stories leave many unanswered questions.

Having been charged on oath, in front of Mr. Joseph Parker JP, by no less a person than Sergeant George Haskins, all of the men, with the exception of Isaac Britton, were conveyed to the city prison in Gloucester, charged with the suspicion of having, on the night of Saturday 27th November 1824, in the parish of Oldland, feloniously assaulted and murdered, one Isaac Garden, to await their trial and their fate that would, almost certainly, be determined not by justice but by prejudice. As for master Britton, he was similarly charged with assault and murder by the police sergeant some four days later, and soon joined his companions in the city gaol.

Back in Warmley, or more precisely Kingswood, witness statements were being taken, and the evidence against the men was being gathered. With seven local men incarcerated in a prison some forty miles away, arrangements had to be made for the witnesses to be taken to Gloucester City where the trial would be held. *ABNER HOWSE*, a farrier by trade, and a part-time Overseer of the Poor, was elected to be the escort to the witnesses, in conjunction with police Sergeant George Haskins, who was ordered to group these persons together, and to take them to and from the Gloucester Assize Courts, and to maintain them whilst in that city, for as little cost as possible. As a prelude to the thrift of the local authority, Abner Howse was made the custodian of £30, to meet these expected costs. Exactly how this money was allocated is not noted, but in addition to the £30 (around £32,500 by today's standards), John Brain, the owner of the land on which Francis Britton's horse strayed, was paid an additional 6/- [0.30p] for two extra days, a *WILLIAM HISCOCKS* was also given the same amount, whilst *SAMUEL FUSSELL,* the landlord of the *Tennis Court Inn* received no less than an extra 15/- [0.75p] for a further five days. Exactly why these three men were paid the extra money will have to remain a mystery, but perhaps they were considered to be the prime witnesses, and were required to be kept by the court, until the trial had ended.

The trial, when it started, occurred over many days, with the prosecution claiming that the knife found at the scene had been clearly identified as belonging to Richard England who, a day or so before Isaac Garden's death, had tried to sell it, with its broken blade, to a fourteen year old boy. A wooden post, stained with what was claimed to be blood, was then produced in the court, and identified as being the property of Mrs. M. Fussell, the landlady of the *Tennis Court Inn.* According to her evidence, the post was used by her to support the clothes line she had at the back of the inn, and she was quite certain that she had used the post during the day of the alleged murder, although it is a little surprising that she had chosen to hang out her washing at that time when it had been a dreary damp cold November day. The prosecution then drew the Courts attention to the fact that when the constable had examined the scene, he had not only noticed a hollow in the wet ground, where quite obviously the base of the post had been stuck whilst holding up the washing line, but in addition he had clearly seen the marks of two pairs of shoes, which he later identified as having been made by the shoes worn by James Caines and Isaac Britton. How this apparently eagle eyed constable had been able to distinguish these particular shoe prints was never established, as ostensibly no one appears to have questioned the constable on this particular point. Reason dictates that, as the washing was not on the line at the time of Isaac Garden's death, then it is likely the damp apparel had, presumably, been previously removed, by Mrs. Fussell, or one of her staff, accordingly would the clothes post therefore have been put back in the same position, and what about the footprints of the person who removed the washing, additionally, with so many people visiting the scene of the killing, during the early hours of the morning, anyone of them could have trampled the site, the constable studied. With most shoes at that time made of leather, the chances of there being any form of pattern showing on the sole of the shoe is quite remote, thus the only identifiable marks that could have been left in the mud, would be size and wear, and accordingly we are left wondering if once again, the Court was exposed to the word of an over zealous constable. There is of course one other possibility that does not appear to have been taken into consideration, which is, that both James and Isaac had quite innocently walked through the lane earlier in the day of the killing, and may have easily have left their shoe prints in the ground near to the base of the clothes post, there is after all no way of telling whether such a print was made before, at the time of, or after the death of Isaac Garden. In addition the constable also claimed that the print of one of James Caines' shoes could be clearly seen close to the opposite hedge, adjacent to where the body was found. Again it is almost certain the Caines and others walked through the lane on the day of the murder, and therefore it would seem abnormal not to have found such a footprint, but how accurately was it identified against Caines' own shoe, was there sufficient evidence to convince a jury that the imprint was made at the time of the attack on the pound keeper; the probable answer to the last point is no, but was James Caines Bush given the benefit of the doubt?

More circumstantial evidence was given later in the trial by the constabulary, which claimed that at the edge of the roadside, ~ exact location not recorded, but presumably along Grimsbury Lane near the stile, ~ they came across a muddy impression of where a man had sat down on the bank, which ran alongside the hedge, whilst resting his feet against the side of the drainage ditch. Clearly showing in the rain-soaked ground was a track of shoe prints, which apparently showed a distinctive shape of where they had been previously repaired, and which led from the pathway to the spot where the man had sat down. Further investigation showed that the distinctive shape was identical to the shoes worn by Mark Whiting, and that in addition there was the damming evidence of the impression left on the bank. To preserve this vital piece of evidence, the constable had dug-up the clay soil impression, and kept it safely secure in a wooden box, which he now presented to the Court, claiming that the impression matched the corduroy breeches worn by Whiting, even down to the mending patch which had been previously sewn in the seat of the trousers. There was of course no doubting that Whiting had walked along the pathway, and had sat down on the bank, under the hedge, facing out on to Grimsbury Lane, but was this really sound evidence that Whiting either on his own, or with accomplices, killed and murdered Isaac Garden. By today's standards, the probable answer would be *No*, but in this early part of the nineteenth century, when there was no forensic science to fall back upon, and when the word of a police officer was rarely doubted, it is not too difficult to know whom the jury will believe.

As the trial progressed, little evidence appears to have been given against Francis Britton, even though it was he who started the altercation, nor against Thomas Wilmot who, it will be remembered, was the apparent culprit of Isaac Garden having been knocked to the ground. Whilst the pound keeper was not there to point a finger at

Wilmot, there would surely have been witnesses who were in the bar room at the time that Garden returned to the inn and made his accusation. In addition nothing whatsoever appears to have been said in court regarding Samuel Peacock, the seventh member of the drinking group. Accordingly it was becoming more and more obvious that the prosecution were concentrating their efforts on Caines, and Whiting who, not being represented by a lawyer, resorted to the only defence they knew, blame the other man and hope to be acquitted in the process.

Mark Whiting claimed that he had known Isaac Garden for at least the past twelve years, and as a friend they had spent many drinking hours in each others company, without a bad word spoken between them. As such, he asserted, he would have absolutely no reason to harm Mr. Garden, let alone murder him. Less fluent in speech, James Caines said very little in his defence, other than to repeat that he was not responsible for the death of the pound keeper.

With the prosecution having rested its case, and with the seven men standing in the dock, the Judge somehow managed to take just over three hours to sum up the case, and whilst his words have not been recorded, it is hard to believe that there was not at times a prejudicial slant to many of his words, particularly as having instructed the jury to retire, and consider the facts put before them, the twelve good men and true took less than ten minutes to come up with the following verdicts:

Francis Britton. [aged 42; described in the Felons Register as being a labourer, 5ft.3ins tall, with a pale complexion and rather stout; he was unable to read or write.] The man who had started the bullying of Isaac Garden because he had disagreed with Garden when the pound keeper had charged Britton to enable his horse to be released from the pound.   NOT GUILTY.

Isaac Britton. [aged 18] Identified, according to the police report in to their study/observation of the shoe prints, as having been, with James Caines Bush, near to the place where the base of the clothes line post had caused, during its use, an indentation in the ground, the same post, it was alleged, which probably caused the fatal blow to the base of Isaac Garden's skull. NOT GUILTY.

James Caines (alias Bush). [aged 19; described in the Felons Register as being just over 5ft 4ins tall, with brown hair, grey eyes, a dark complexion, and a full face with several visible scars resulting from his employment as a collier; he could neither read nor write.] Identified with Isaac Britton as having been near to the place where the clothes post had caused the indentation, the same post that the police claimed to have been splashed with blood, and which was, in their opinion, the weapon used to strike the fatal blow, although how such an unwieldy instrument was used, without hitting others was never explained. For the post to be an effective prop of the clothes line, it would have needed to be at least seven foot long, and could quite easily have been as long as eight feet. How such a "weapon" could have been swung around in the confines of the hedge bound pathway, let alone be accurately aimed at the back of someone's head in the misty darkness of that November night, was never considered, or discussed in any way, let alone be put to any form of test. As far as the police were concerned, blood had been splattered on the post, and accordingly it must have been the murder weapon. Apart from the circumstantial evidence of believing that the police were capable of identifying and isolating footprints that matched Caines' shoes, nothing further was presented; nevertheless the verdict pronounced by the Jury was GUILTY AS CHARGED.

Samuel Peacock. [aged 21; described in the Felons Register as 5ft 4ins tall, a cordwainer by trade, with a pale complexion, a long face, with a large nose, and a scar on his forehead; he could both read and write.] Little is known of this man's involvement with the altercation at the *Tennis Court Inn,* or with the subsequent events, and accordingly he was found   NOT GUILTY.

Robert England. [aged 20; described in the Felons Register as just under 5ft 1ins tall ~ the shortest of the seven men ~ a collier by trade, with an oval shaped face, which was very much marked by the after effects of having suffered smallpox.] Known to be the owner of the clasp knife found at the scene of the crime, where Garden's body had not only been found with a terrible fracture to the base of his skull, but also had two stab wounds to the head, likely to have been made with the blade of a knife. However, connecting the damaged knife found at the scene of the crime with these two stab wounds seemed to be beyond the comprehension of the local constabulary, as no further investigation was made into this item, and the matter was hardly raised at the trial.   NOT GUILTY

Mark Whiting. [aged 22; described in the Felons Register as being a labourer, 5ft 4ins tall with brown hair and brown eyes, able to read a little, but not able to write.] This young man, described as having come from a better family class, and better educated than his drinking companions, appears to have been unlucky to have sat down, on a patch of damp clay close to the vicinity of the murder scene, at the time he was wearing corduroy breeches, which had quite recently been patched by his mother. As such, the police were able to readily jump to the conclusion, that having matched the seat of the trousers with the muddy imprint then, not only was Whiting there, he was also responsible for the death of the pound keeper, as no other explanation was considered or sought.   GUILTY AS CHARGED.

Thomas Wilmot. [aged 19] Accused by Isaac Garden of having followed him out of the pub, and then assaulted and knocked him to the ground not long after he had left the *Tennis Court Inn* for the first time. NOT GUILTY.

Almost 180 years after the event, it is difficult to make a sound judgement on exactly what went on and what was said at the trial of these seven men, or what went on in the minds of the twelve good men and true. That they were influenced by undoubted prejudicial details given by the police and the prosecution, without any scientific basis, or alternative possibilities being considered goes without saying, as does the fact that however honest and upright the members of the jury were, they were all likely to have been drawn from the property owning classes, better educated, and most likely to be intolerant and prejudgmental of the lower working classes. The fact that it took the presiding judge to take over three hours to "instruct" the jury may indicate that he was being fair minded and was putting over the various benefits of the doubt on behalf of the defendants, but if he was why did it only take the jurors ten minutes to come up with their conclusions. In addition, why was there an apparent emphasise on Caines and Whiting, but in addition how could the damning evidence against England appear to have been ignored, what about the demon drink and its effect on say Francis Britton, and Thomas Wilmot who is the only one to have actually assaulted Garden, surely in the mind of most jurors, if two of the seven were guilty, then all seven were probably guilty, unless of course they were greatly influenced by the judge himself. There are unfortunately, decisions taken in today's Court Rooms that are hard to understand, and perhaps the decision taken in this case falls into the same category of being unsafe, and that the conclusion of the jurors was prejudicial and wrong.

Having given their verdicts on the seven men, Francis, Isaac, Robert, Samuel and Thomas were set free, leaving just James and Mark in the dock to receive their fate, ~ to be hanged by the neck until dead.

On the 11th April 1825, just three days after the conclusion of the trial the prison chaplain walked ahead of a composed James Caines Bush and a composed Mark Whiting, both of whom were hand-cuffed, and had chains around their ankles, as they shuffled from their cells to the scaffold over the gate house. With a black hood placed over their heads, they were invited to stand over the trap door in the floor, and to meet their maker.

Although in the past, hanged sons of Bitton were, very often brought "home" to be buried, this privilege was not accorded to either James or Mark, and the position of their final resting place is something of a mystery. There appears to be no trace of their burial in the prison records, and at the request of their families, the incumbent of St. Mary's Bitton, Canon Ellacombe, wrote to the prison governor for details, but the latter's reply simply gave a date of disposal and no further details. In these circumstances it would seem most likely that the cruellest act in this tragic story was probably played by the authorities who allowed the bodies of these young men to be sold to the medical profession who were always on the look out for bodies to be dissected, and examined, especially healthy ones.

* * * * *

Having presented her common-law husband with a son in 1805, Betty gave birth to a second son two years later who was christened *FRANCIS CAINES BUSH* as Betty, no doubt, wished to carry over into the next generation, the memory of her older brother's name, who had be hanged just three years previously. As with all of the children there is no record of Francis' life as he grew up and matured into manhood, but almost certainly he was well taught in the art and nature of crime, as he was, no doubt, frequently reminded that it was necessary for him to live up to the established and fanciful reputation of the uncle after whom he was named. Like his brother James at the relatively early age of six years, he suffered the loss of having his father forcibly taken away from him, when Timothy Bush was sent to the other side of the world, and then not long afterwards, he had to cope with the introduction of a surrogate father when George Groves moved in with his mother, and within a year his mother had had yet another son, a step brother to deal with.

Two years later, aged eight, his mother's oldest brother followed his father to the colonies and, if not to be outdone, a further two years later Francis was to lose yet another uncle when, at the age of ten, his mother's younger brother Thomas was also sentenced to be transported. If that was not enough, in the same year his twenty-four year old Uncle Benjamin was hanged. All of these events must have had a very disturbing affect on one so young, in particular one whose probable upbringing had revolved around the need to be strong, tough and hard as part of his reincarnation with the uncle after whom he was named, and this no doubt meant that tears were not to be shed, even though a favourite uncle had been hanged, and then buried with that uncle with whom he shared a name.

By the time he reached his teenage years, Francis was already involved in petty crime, and at the tender age of fourteen, he was charged with the theft of stealing chickens and, having been found guilty, he was sentenced to twenty-eight days detention in prison.

The following year, Francis was back to his old tricks, and on this occasion the sentence for having stolen three or four hens was to be privately whipped with twenty-five lashes.

The year 1823 was either a quiet year in his criminal activities, or he was lucky enough not to have been caught, but the time was not wasted as Francis continued to hone his skills, and to widen his horizons, away from the more mundane activities of stealing poultry, even if the latter did mean that a substantial meal was very often the end result. By now Francis was a strong young man, who was full of his own abilities, and immortality and, having acquired a horse he was free to spread his wings beyond the much narrower confines of his brother's behaviour and desires. His brother James, could scratch a living by hacking coal beneath the surface, and to supplement his meagre income by carrying out the occasional theft, but as far as Francis was concerned he was after bigger "fish" and intended with his friend *SAMUEL NEEDS* to seek out his victims as they travelled along the king's highway. To start with both men only dabbled in their newfound sport, picking on the poor, and those who were less likely to complain to the authorities that they had been robbed, but by the middle of 1824 they were becoming flushed with success, and bolder in their attacks. As so often happens, their boldness soon turned into recklessness and as 1824 turned into 1825, the men were tracked down, arrested and charged on oath with the felonious crime of highway robbery.

Within days of their arrest, both men were sent to Gloucester City prison to await trial, the same prison, which was also at that time the domicile of Francis' elder brother James, held on the charge of the unlawful death of Isaac Garden. Whether either brother knew of the other's incarceration in the same prison can only be guessed at, but by a strange quirk of fate, the trial of Francis and Samuel was held on the day after James walked to the scaffold, and thus for the poor mother left in Bitton, there was the dreadful knowledge of knowing that her first born had been hanged on the 11th April 1825, whilst her second child was, on the 12th April 1825, being sentenced to be transported for life; this sentence being carried out on the 6th December 1825, when on board the sailing vessel *Woodman* Francis left these shores for the very last time bound for Van Diemen's Land.

The tragic events, which surround these two brothers, received little if any sympathy at the time, with the following report appearing in an April edition of the *Gloucester Journal.*

"The name of Caines has for years been notorious in this county and the majority of them have either been hanged or transported. It would seem as if the severe visitation of the law could have no effect in checking the propensity to crime, which pervades this depraved family."

Very obviously the journalist had no sympathy for the family, and was quite clearly prepared to perpetuate the theme of giving a "dog a bad name". However, it must be remembered that his newspaper was only read by the middle and upper classes, whose extremely low opinion and attitude to the members of the working class meant that they would certainly agree that the Caines and any other such degraded person had simply got their just desserts, and that it was quite beneath their dignity to have any form of compassion for such dreadful people.

* * * * *

As already noted, within a matter of weeks after Timothy Bush was transported in 1813, Betty had begun a new liaison with George Groves, and soon found herself pregnant again, giving birth, during 1814, to a third son *THOMAS CAINES GROVES,* presumably deciding once again to name her child after one of her brothers. No doubt like his stepbrothers, Thomas was introduced to the family practice at quite an early age, and like all of the Caines children there are no records in existence relating to his childhood. His father George appears to have looked after his stepsons equally as well as he looked after his own son during the nine years or so that they were all together. During that time Betty had to cope with two brothers having been hanged, and two brothers, and her first common law husband, having been transported, whilst at the same time she was bringing up her three sons and dealing with her second "husbands" criminal activities. Then during 1822, the inevitable happened, George Groves was caught and also sent to the other side of the world. Within three years of this event, Betty somehow had to deal with the further tragedies of having her eldest son being hanged, and her second son following in his father's footsteps. In the meanwhile throughout this cataclysm of events, Thomas was continuing to grow towards his teenage years, whilst being influenced and affected by every dreadful twist of the tale. By now Thomas had to all intents and purposes, dropped his father's family name, and was more often than not simply known as Thomas Caines, or Thomas Caines alias Groves.

Mother and son remained together over the following six years or more, during which time Betty was undoubtedly subsidized by the remnants of her family, and by the theft of food, either in the form of poultry, or grain, or root vegetables, by young Thomas. With the problems of the past behind them, almost certainly and most understandably, Betty and Thomas kept a low profile, and as far as can be determined, they were able to escape any prosecution from their self-survival instincts. As always happens, either their luck ran out, or Thomas became too cocksure and full of his own importance, or it was just one theft too many as, in 1832 at the age of eighteen, Thomas was arrested and charged with theft. By the time that Thomas came before the Magistrates sitting at the Gloucester City Summer Assizes of 1832, he had just passed his nineteenth birthday, and was recorded as being a labourer by trade. Bearing in mind that this was the first occasion when he had appeared before any magistrate, he was extremely harshly treated, inasmuch as he received absolutely no lenience from the upper class bench who sat in judgment with or without justice. No doubt recognising the name Caines, and the obviously depraved family from which he, Thomas, must have come, they considered, although in reality they probably never gave it a second thought, that the only option they had was to sentence this young man to transportation for life. Accordingly, on the 22nd September 1832, Betty's youngest son followed in the footsteps of his father, his brother, and his mother's first "husband" when he boarded the sailing vessel *Camden* bound for New South Wales. Having left these shores for good, he undertook his punishment as stoically as he could, and was ultimately rewarded with his freedom. Sometime during the early 1840's, he became a publican in Liverpool Street, Holbart, and gave the pub the prosaic name *"HELP ME THROUGH THE WORLD",* let us hope that it did.

#####

THE PARTNERS AND CHILDREN OF LYDIA CAINES

It is almost certain that Lydia had separate liaisons with at least three men, although that is not to say that she lived with each one. At the age of eighteen, Lydia gave birth to a son who was christened *GEORGE CAINES AVERY,* thus confirming the father's family name, but not his own first name. Like all of his cousins, emphasis was put on the use of his mother's maiden name, and the practise of learning as much as he could with regard to the world of trifling and not so trifling crime. At probably around eight years of age of years, George was apprenticed with a local hat maker or hat dyer, and over the following five years or so George was able to carry on this training, earning a small pittance for his efforts. Whether or not it was in the blood, or just a major symptom of his environment will never be established, but for George, the idea of scraping a living from hat dyeing was simply not an option particularly when much more money could be made from the consuming need to use the more developed skills, he had learned from a baby. By all accounts, George took to theft in quite a big way, for he certainly appears to have had quite fine grandiose ideas about the scale of his nocturnal activities. Little is known of him and, as far as can be determined in the local records, he escaped the clutches of the law for most of the time he plied his illegal trade, which is somewhat surprising as George believed in robbing not so much the poor, but the rich, and usually they cherished their money and their property with such great diligence, that woe betide anyone who tried to separate their assets from them. However, all good things must come to an end, and in George's case this occurred some time during 1832/33 when he had the audacity to consider, and subsequently execute a substantial burglary on William Blathwayt's house at Dyrham Park. Having gained entry, despite the numerous servants on duty, his haul included, 1-silver tankard; 12-silver dress buckles; 30-shirts; 1- gold brooch, gold seals, rings and other articles, with a total value of £4-500. Although he was able to remove these items from the house, and from the surrounding parkland without being seen or caught, there was such a hue and cry over the impertinence of his crime, and the value of the property taken that every available constable was put on the hunt to catch the perpetrator. Coming from the background he did, there was not much of a demand for silver buckles, or gold brooches, and as for the fine linen shirts, they were most unlikely to stand up to the rigors of working class life. Thus however successful George had been in carrying out the theft, what he was left with was too many "hot potatoes" to handle, and a huge embarrassment of unwanted goodies. Whether it was down to George suddenly appearing to have unexpected wealth, or whether he unwisely tried to "sell" the items to those who would not be discrete remains hidden, all that is known is that within a relatively short while of having carried out the robbery, George was arrested and sent for trial. At the subsequent hearing, George was found guilty and although he had no previously proven convictions, he did have an "Achilles' heel" which shone through any defence he may have offered, and that was his preponderance to use the family name Caines. Sentenced at the August Assizes to be transported for life, George was held in a hulk for the next four months before being taken to the sailing vessel *Hive* on the 29th January 1834, bound for the penal colony in New South Wales.

With his departure, the long and somewhat sad story of the felonious Caines family virtually came to an end. Of those members of the family still left in the area, only a few continued to get into trouble with the law, and in all cases, the trouble seemed to have been no more than minor misdemeanours. Obviously, after sixty years or more of being in the criminal highlight, the family name continued to attract rumours, counter rumours, and accusations, all of which needed to be lived down as the years rolled by. However, it is believed that Lydia gave birth to another son during or around 1815, who was given the first name *EDWARD*, and with his father unrecorded, the family name Caines.

Like most of the Caines, little if anything is known about them other than when they crossed the path of the law keepers, or appeared in court, and such is the case as far as Edward is concerned. Whether or not he participated in minor petty crimes is unknown, for if he did then he must have got away with it, as there are no records of any convictions. What has been recorded is that during 1842, Edward was drinking in a public house somewhere in the City of Bath, and that during the evening there was an altercation with one or two other patrons. Exactly what started the dispute was not identified, but according to Edward, he was the subject of cruel taunts about his surname, and about the reputation his family had for being rough tough, and hard. Trying not to respond to the taunts, Edward found himself more and more isolated, and it was not long before, the taunts changed into pushing and shoving, then slaps and ultimately fists. Edward claimed that he found himself being "beaten up" and, in self-defence, he drew a knife and turned upon his tormentors. Heavily outnumbered, now that others in the alehouse had joined in, Edward was overpowered, and handed over to members of the local constabulary, who had been called to the scene of the fighting by the landlord. Charged with attempted murder, Edward was sent to trial, to explain why, under the greatest of provocation, he had drawn his knife,

Although the presiding magistrates fully acknowledged the provocation felt by the accused, and despite the fact that Edward had no previous convictions recorded against him, they still felt that they were unable to sympathise with his difficulties, and accordingly sentenced him to be transported to the colonies for a minimum period of seven years. As far as has been recorded no one was seriously hurt by Edward, and almost certainly, he came off much worse, thus whilst he should perhaps not have taken the law into his own hands, it is difficult to see how he could have extricated himself from the altercation with a modicum of personal safety. In such circumstances, a penal sentence of transportation for seven years ~

effectively life, as the chances of him saving sufficient money to return home was virtually impossible ~ seems extremely harsh, and totally unnecessary, and was surely based upon the further prejudicial nature of the presiding magistrates who obviously felt that having once given a dog a bad name, that that was sufficient reason alone to send Edward Caines to the other side of the world.

########

BENJAMIN CAINES = ANN COOL
BORN 1757   BORN C1759
MARRIED 1777 ST MARY'S BITTON

GEORGE	FRANCIS	ELIZABETH	BENJAMIN	THOMAS	ROBERT	LYDIA	BENJAMIN	SAMUEL	SARAH	JOSEPH
b 1777	b 1779	b 1781	b 1784	b 1786	b 1788	b 1790	b 1793	b 1795	b 1798	b 1803

Elizabeth = Timothy Bush

Lydia = ? Avery

Samuel = Hannah

Children of Elizabeth & Timothy Bush:
- JAMES CAINES BUSH b 1805
- FRANCIS CAINES BUSH b 1807

Children of Lydia & Avery:
- GEORGE CAINES AVERY b 1808
- EDWARD CAINES b 1815

Children of Samuel & Hannah:
- MARY b 1817
- ANN b 1820
- ELIZA b 1822

= George Groves

THOMAS CAINES GROVES

INDEX

Alberry Thomas (alias Maggs)   70

Baker James   71
Baker William   70
Ballard Isaac   71
Batman William   50
Batt Moses   46/51
Batt Thomas   32
Bevan Thomas   49/55
Brain John   79
Brain Samuel   51
Brain Samuel (alias Black)   70
Britton Frank   (Francis) 26/27/28/70/78-96
Britton George   70
Britton Hester   51
Britton Isaac   78-96
Britton Lydia   21
Britton Samuel   50
Britton Stephen   52
Bryant Dennis   50
Bryant James.   12/64/65/69
Bryant Joseph   50/71
Bryant Samuel   50
Bryant William   50
Bull Charles   46/51
Bush Elizabeth   77
Bush Francis Caines   38/41/97
Bush Giles   77
Bush James Caines   38/41/78-96
Bush Timothy   38/39/40/43/97

Caines Abigail.   19
Caines Abraham.   19/20
Caines Alexander   24
Caines Ann   24
Caines Ann daughter of Samuel   72/75
Caines Benjamin Snr   21
Caines Benjamin Jnr   21/24/43
Caines Benjamin, son of Benjamin Jnr.
   37/44/47/49/55/56/57/61/62/63/64/66-70
Caines Benjamin son of Samuel   22/23/24
Caines Benjamin   21/22
Caines Edward   103/104
Caines Eliza   72/75
Caines Elizabeth (Betty)   38/42/43/44/54/58
Caines Francis   32/35/36/44/62
Caines George   26/27/28/30/31/44/45/54/62
Caines George (alias Avery)   58/102/103
Caines Hannah   72

Groves George   40/41/42/97/100
Garden (Gorden) Isaac   78-96
Green Joseph   23

Haskins George   86/88
Hathaway George   38
Hathway James   51
Hawkins Susannah   21/22
Hiscocks William   89
Hobbs Richard   10
Howse Abner   89

Isles Abraham   14/15/16
Isles Moses   10

Jefferis William   23
Jones Hannah   51

Kaynes Abraham   18
Kaynes Andrew   18
Kaynes Thomas   18
Kaynes William Snr.   18
Kaynes William Jnr.   18

Lacey Sarah   51
Lacey William   51
Lewis Henry   10
Lewis Isaac
Lewis Mrs.   87
Little George   74

Monk?   64
Moreton Henry   70
Moreton Richard   70

Needs Samuel   98
Nichol Hannah   25

Owen Moses   54

Caines Jane   19
Caines Jane daughter of Samuel   74
Caines Jeane   18
Caines Joseph   72/76
Caines Joshua   24
Caines Lydia   57/58/60
Caines Lucy   24
Caines Mary Snr.   19
Caines Mary Jnr.   19
Caines Mary daughter of Richard   25
Caines Mary daughter of Samuel   22/72/75
Caines Mary daughter of Thomas   24
Caines Richard   21/24/25
Caines Robert son of Benjamin Jnr.   57
Caines Robert son of Samuel   22
Caines Samuel   19/21/22/25/72/73/75/76
Caines Sarah daughter of Benjamin   72/76
Caines Sarah daughter of Richard   25
Caines Sarah daughter of Thomas   24
Caines Thomas   21/23/24/25
Caines Thomas, son of Benjamin Jnr.
   45/46/47/49/54/55/56/61
Caines Thomas (alias Groves)   40/100
Cooke Samuel   50/71
Cool Ann   24
Cox Isaac   29 /38
Cribb Benjamin   71
Cribb Isaac   38/46/47/48
Cribb James   54/55
Cribb Robert   50/51
Cribb Thomas   50
Curtis Benjamin   29/30/46

Dolling Mr. of Cold Ashton   55

England Robert   60/78-96
Ettle John   71
Ettle Joseph   71
Evans James   63/64/65

Francis James   30
Frankcomb E.   53
Fry Abraham   22
Fry George   13
Fry John   51
Fry Joseph   13
Fry Sampson   22/50
Fry William   10
Fuller Charles   32/33
Fussell Mrs. M   89/90
Fussell Samuel   89

Palmer Mr. of Keynsham   54
Parker Joseph (alias Evans)   71
Parker Joseph JP   85/88
Peacock Edward   10/70
Peacock George   24
Peacock Samuel   78-96
Peake Edward   10
Phipps Henry   71
Ponting Mrs.   87
Porter Jacob   10
Powe William   51
Powell Ann   53

Powell Joseph   53
Pratten Thomas   71
Prigg Sarah   62/64/66

Read John   11

Scull Abraham   14/16
Snellgrove William   40
Stephens Elizabeth   36
Sweet Thomas   70

Thompson George   10
Townsend Mary   51

Ward George   12/13
Ward John   11
Ward Samuel   13
Webb Benjamin   12/13
Webb Robert   14/16
Whiting Mark   78-96
Whittuck Samuel   5/6
Willis Ambrose   51
Willis Henry   51/71
Willis Joseph   39/40/43
Willmott Elizabeth (Betty)   24
Wilmot George   70
Wilmot Giles   70
Wilmot Henry   64/65/69
Wilmot Thomas   39/40/78-96
Wilmott Elizabeth Caines   59
Wilmott James Caines   59/74
Wilmott Jasper   59